The Wheel-Maker's Craft™ Series

Book Two

Guide to Restoring

an Antique

SpinningWheel

Carson Cooper

Other books in The Wheel-Maker's Craft™ Series

- Guide to Making Spinning Wheel Flyers and Wheels

- Guide to Making Spinning Wheels, Plans and Instructions for Building Saxony, Irish Castle and Accelerator Wheels

The Wheel-Maker's Craft™ Series

Book Two

Guide to Restoring

an Antique

SpinningWheel

Carson Cooper

Cooper Smith Publishing

Guide to Restoring an Antique Spinning Wheel

Author photo: by KJT

Library of Congress Control Number: 2008905898
ISBN 978-0-9818772-1-1

Manufactured in the United States of America

Cooper Smith Publishing
P.O. Box 66554
Scotts Valley, CA 95067
www.Ztwist.com

CONTENTS

To best friends and trusted shop-helpers.

"SPINNING, the act or art of reducing filk, flax, hemp, wool, hair, or other matters into thread. ... Hemp, flax, nettle-thread, and the like vegetable matters, are to be wetted in fpinning ; filks, wools, etc., are to be fpun dry..."[1]

—Dictionary of Arts and Sciences, 1771

Chapter One

In the Days of the Wheel Maker

N early two hundred years have past since the spinning wheel gave up its reign; quickly replaced by the clang and clatter of the Industrial Age. So many wheels were left in the wake that even now these are found in a number of venues. Many of these wheels bear evidence of extensive use; highlighting the superb skills possessed by spinners and makers alike.

The grooves on this flyer arm tell a tale of the daily life of our ancestors.

From inventory records of the years 1656 through 1795, it has been shown that a majority of the population had spinning wheels and looms in the home. Those with spinning wheels alone numbered as much as eighty percent of the population. In many countries these wheels served as a source of secondary income to help the families through the winter months.[2]

The Wheel Maker's Trade

The sheer numbers of wheels in use during this period provided a thriving industry for turners of the day. Wheels, reels, looms, flax hackles, all required special skills to make, as did the ever required maintenance on such tools. Bergeron, in 1792, writes that: "reels [bobbins] and hecks [flyers] can be obtained almost anywhere."[3] Joseph Moxon gives an interesting reference to bobbin making in his *Mechanick Exercises* published in 1703.[4] Later works indicate this was a staple trade for turners well into the late 19th century.

Records of the encouragement of linen trade in Europe have preserved a window into the occupation of the wheel maker. The budget sheet (from an investment to promote public employment) shown in Fig. 1.1, allows for a look at the wheel maker's [wheelwright] position during the height of the spinning-wheel's rule. Interestingly, the wheelwright's pay exceeded that of the weaver, but not that of the hackler. Hackling was hard work.

Estimated annual support for new manufacturing stations (£ = pounds sterling, s. = shillings)	£	s.
1. For purchasing lint-seed to be distributed for sowing, a sum not exceeding ...	20	0
2. For prizes to be given among the raisers of the greatest and best quantities of flax, a sum not exceeding ...	3	0
3. For a salary to a hackler, a sum not exceeding ...	30	0
4. For a salary to a **wheelwright**, a sum not exceeding ...	20	0
5. For a salary to a spinning-mistress, and for furnishing, firing, candle, and other necessities to the spinning-school, a sum not exceeding ...	28	0
6. Towards defraying the maintenance of the scholars at the spinning-school, a sum not exceeding ...	48	0
7 For purchasing wheels and reels to be distributed among the scholars after they are instructed, and other proper persons in the neighbourhood of the station, a sum not exceeding ...	50	0
8. For prizes to be given among the spinners in the neighbourhood of the station, a sum not exceeding ...	4	8
9. For a salary to a weaver, a sum not exceeding ...	15	0
10. Towards defraying the maintenance of apprentices with the hackler, wheelwright, and weaver, for the second year of their apprenticeships, a sum not exceeding ...	30	0
11. To a principal undertaker, for providing flax to the people at the station and neighbourhood, to be spun, and for defraying the charge of freight and carriage and other extraordinary expenses at the station, a sum not exceeding ...	100	0
Making in whole for each station	£348	8

Fig 1.1 ➤ From a *1753 Act for improving manufactures in Scotland.* [5]

Hand Spinning and Early Economics

Many thousands of wheels were distributed during the 17th and 18th century, by government and private enterprise, to encourage textile production. The Linen Board in Ireland is said to have spent £3,000 annually on spinning-wheels; up to the time when England ultimately converted to machine spinning. At that time, six thousand wheels could be purchased for the sum. Its seems nostalgia may have been a factor in the Board's final distribution of two thousand new wheels; this, after machinery had achieved the ability to spin yarn as fine as previously only possible by hand.[6]

While much of the materials used in making cloth were produced locally, trade was extensive. Empires were made from the trade of these manufactures; controlling the wealth that came from the monopolies of wool, linen, hemp, and cotton was a very complicated endeavour. While trade was usually very profitable, at times it became necessary to rein in the amount of certain goods being exported.

By the 14th century restrictions on the exporting of English wool are found with many more thereafter. The following from a speech given to the Commons (during the reign of Henry VII), painted an underlying sentiment found repeated for several centuries: "His Grace prays you take into consideration matter of trade as also the manufactures of the kingdom... and likewise that our people be set

Wool varies greatly depending on the breed of sheep. Many breeds were based on the Spanish Merino (shown at left).

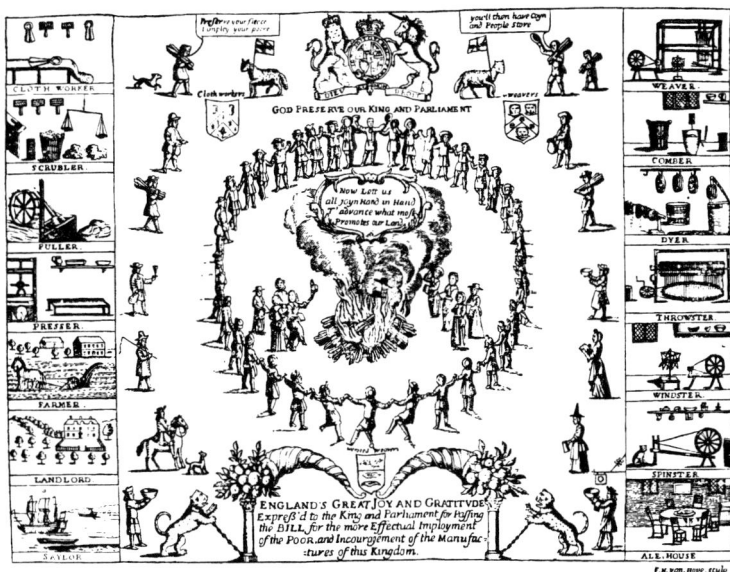

Broadside from the late 1600's.[7] Expressing the sentiment "preserve your fleece and employ your poore [sic]." Social responsibilities, as well as improvement of commerce, spawned many such ventures.

on work in arts and handicrafts, that the realm may subsist more of itself, that idleness be avoided, and the draining out of our treasures for foreign manufactures stopped." [8]

Throughout the time of the spinning-wheel, the making of cloth was one method used to ease the condition of poverty; arising from famine and the ever-changing social and political conditions. At a time in England's history when improving manufactures in the textile industries was an important issue, England was also faced with: What to do with her large population of homeless and poor?

The growing, harvesting, and processing of flax and hemp provided plenty of work for the people who wished to pursue it.

"This," said she, *"is the most useful thing you have found; lose not a moment in searching for more of these leaves, and bring me the most you can of them; I will make you stockings, shirts, clothes, thread, ropes --- In short, give me Flax, looms, and frames, and I shall be at no loss in the employment of it."* [9]

—Swiss Family Robinson

The Textile Fibres

Flax— One of the most useful members of the plant world, it is actually the stem of the plant which makes flax so versatile a material. There are two primary uses for flax and hemp: first, for the fibers used in cloth manufacture, second, for the seed which has many uses.

Thin-Leafed Wild Flax
Linum Angustifolium

Belonging to the order *Linaceæ*, the flax plant is that from which linen yarns are produced. While there are over one hundred species of flax, the one from which linen is produced is *Linum usitatissimum*. This variety is said to be the ancient flax of Egypt and Assyria, a more ancient species, *L. angustifolium* is the plant used by the Swiss Lake Dwellers.

Hemp
Cannabis Sativus

Hemp—Belonging to the Mulberry family, *Moraceæ*, the species *Cannabis Sativa* includes several strains of hemp having very different uses.[10] Fiber producing hemp grown in America was introduced from England in 1632. The use of hemp dates back to at least 2700 B.C. in China where some of the most

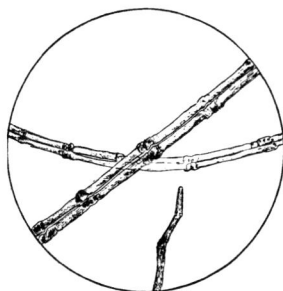

desirable fiber producing strains were cultivated. These began replacing the European strain in America around 1857.[11] The fiber of the plants (used for spinning) consists of long strands of overlapping cells in the inner bark, or bast, of the stalk.

Bast fibre.
—Matthews, *The Textile Fibres*

Regarding hemp: it must be noted that the European strains, used for fiber, are not the same as that which is cultivated for the narcotic effects; the latter originating in India and Africa. The foliage of the India strain is much denser and has a "nearly solid stalk." The strains which are used for fiber production generally have a stalk of which—one half is hollow.[12]

Cultivation of both flax, and hemp was common-place in colonial America. From Virginia in 1649, one writer states: "They begin to plant much Hempe [sic] and Flax which they find growes [sic] well and good."[13] While many types of hemp plants have been used for making yarn, most are best used for coarse cloth and cordage. Suitable for textiles "requiring strength and bulk" hemp provides a long lasting garment fabric.

While once not common to find a complete garment made from hemp fibers, it was certainly a common material for buckram and canvas. Primarily made from hemp, buckram was gummed and pressed smooth, by a process called calendering, then dyed. Used as a liner in a variety of garments where a stiff material, that could keep its form well, might be needed; it was also used as a protective wrapping material. Hemp buckram appears to have had a considerable market in Europe in the 18th century. Hemp is well known for its use in sail canvas for shipping, but much was also used (unbleached) for domestic purposes such as towels, and as a backing for tapestry work.[14]

Nettle—The nettle is another of the plants actually used for cloth; cultivated in Germany as well as the province of Picardy in France, and to some extent Sweden. Known also as Swedish hemp, its use was primarily for cordage there. The stinging nettles *Urtica urena* and *Urtica dioica* are two of several species of nettle which have been used. *Utica urena* has the smaller fibers of the two mentioned, and closely resembles linen fibers.

In Germany the cloth woven from nettle was called *Nesseltuch* and could be bleached pure white, much as linen.[15] Throughout the many wars in Europe's past, interruption of imports between neighboring countries forced the use of whatever resources were available. Nettle was one of the alternatives at hand and was used in place of flax when that was not available.

Common Nettle
Urtica Dioica

Fibers from Stems

The first process of separating the filaments of bast fibers, from the outer woody portion of the stem, is called retting. This consists of making the substance holding the fibers together soluble, allowing removal by secondary treatments. Retting was traditionally done by submersion in water; another method was laying the fibers out for the morning dew to moisten. Varying results are obtained, often the desired color and use of the fibre define which is used. Dew retting of flax requires a couple of weeks, yields a darker color (a silvery gray), with less even results. Water retted flax requires a soft water, and timely removal from submersion when the fermentation process is complete.

OCCUPATION, in a legal fenfe, is taken for ufe or tenure ; as in deeds it is frequently faid, ... It is likewise used for a trade or myftery. [16]

The Wheel Makers

While all this growth in the textile trades was promoted, the men who made the tools needed to produce the cloth is largely the silent trade in history. The occupations of the 11th through 18th centuries were often varied between domestic work and that of an artisan. In the case of the weavers and hand-spinners, before the factory replaced domestic manufacture, many were also farmers. The makers of the tools for textile production were little different in this respect.

Sometimes called "little-wheel" makers, these men had a wide range of skills which farmers of the day needed to survive. Well versed in the forging of iron and working of wood, these men were often known as *mechanics* or *mechanicians*. Until the late 19th century this title was used to describe those able to fabricate what ever they required, using a hammer and forge, trusty foot lathe, and a set of files.

The *mysteries of wheel-making* were often taught starting when the student was around fourteen years of age; some served an apprenticeship, though many times the skills were passed on to the son of a practicing wheel-maker. Often, a grandfather had been a weaver and farmer, the father a wheel-maker and farmer, with the son taking over the making of spinning-wheels. Since the late 15th century such stories are to be found. Two families which serve as examples are: the Farnhams of New England, and (one with an older history) the Forsters of England.

Joel Farnham is known to have been born in Windham, Connecticut in 1774. Settling in Tioga County, New York he established a carding mill there and began making wheels at about twenty years of age. When his sons Charles and Frederick were of age they began helping in the shop; Frederick carried on the business, making accelerating heads and wheels in the mid 1800's. [17]

On the opposite side of the Atlantic, there are at least three references to different Forsters who made spinning-wheels near Brampton, England. A John Forster (or Forrester), William Forster I, and William Forster II. John Forster (1688-1781) made spinning wheels, sometimes worked as a gun smith and "occasionally made fiddles."[18] William Forster (1713-1801) of Brampton was a respected maker of spinning-wheels, but is most remembered for being an early violin maker. William Forster Sr. had a son in 1739, named after his father. William Forster Jr. followed in the trades of both making spinning-wheels and making violins, with a period as a gun-stock maker in harder times. He finally left the manufacture of spinning-wheels when his reputation as a violin maker began to earn him particular esteem in the art.

Many immigrants to North America listed their trade, in early records, as wheelwrights and turners. As with the Farnhams and Forsters, they "practised [sic] making wheels so long as they were in use in the country" being "put out of use by the invention of machinery." As economic conditions transformed the ability of common folk to make a living, wheel-wrights likely fared a little better than did the spinners and weavers. The lives of these were about to be shaped in a manner that was, most often, less than pleasant.

Credited with a design for a *double flyer* spinning-wheel, the well connected and influential philanthropist Thomas Firmin deserves mention, when speaking of important wheel-makers. Mr. Firmin is known for providing work and instruction in the textile trades to hundreds of poor and homeless. In promoting the social reclamation of the needy (and in the process giving England increased output of textile production) his *Proposals for the Imployment of the Poor* was published in 1681. It was in this publication that his double flyer spinning-wheel design was famously illustrated.

Double flyer wheel

So promising did the use of the double wheel seem to Mr. Firmin's friend, the noted philosopher John Locke, that he introduced it in a proposal to the King. Within his proposal we are given a unique glimpse at the spinning-wheel, and spinner's, importance at the end of the 17th century:

"To hinder, therefore, the growth of the woollen manufacture in Ireland, so wholly incompatible with the fundamental trade of England, on which the prosperity of this nation so much depends, we are humbly of opinion that the exportation of all parts whatsoever (except only that of their frieze, as is wont, to England) be restrained and discouraged with impositions, penalties and all other ways which together may be sufficient to hinder it.

"But since the private exportation of wool in England, acknowledged by everybody to be directly against the interest of this kingdom, though under the severest penalties, are to be depended upon where the temptation of great profit may encourage private men to

bribe officers and run other risks, it is much less to be expected that the bare stopping of the exportation of the exportation of woollen manufactures, when made by a guard only at the ports, will be sufficient to keep them from being sent out of Ireland...

"We, therefore, crave leave humbly to offer to your excellencies' consideration, whether it will not be convenient to add the following remedies as a more natural and effectual way to take off the people there from their applica-tion to that sort of trade, so that the cheapness of victuals and consequently, of labour may not enable them to transport the woolen manufactures to foreign markets to the prejudice of the English trade—

Fuller's Teazel
Dipsacus Fullonum

"That a sufficient duty be laid upon the importation of oil, upon teasles whether imported or growing there, and upon all the utensils employed in the making of woolen manufactures, such as cards for wool of all sorts, fulling mills, racks, presses, etc., as also the uten-sils of woolen combers, and particularly a duty by the yard upon all cloth and woolen stuffs (except friezes) before they are taken off the loom...

'That the present customs and other duties on hemp, flax and all manufactures made thereof, imported into Ireland, be increased one-fourth part every year, till they come to be quadrupled to what they are at present, and that the like graduate increase of duties be laid on calicoes and all other sorts of cloth made of cotton that may supply the place and use of linen.

" That the exportation of linen cloth and all other manufactures made of flax or hemp, without any mixture of wool, shall be free to all places and without any custom.

"That all dressers of hemp or flax, linen weavers, rope-makers, and all other workers, in hemp or flax, and using no other trades, shall

be free, during the time that they follow those vocations, from serv
ing of juries or bearing any offices which they themselves shall not be
willing to undergo.

" And, because the poorest earning in the several parts of the linen
manufacture is at present in the work of the spinners, who therefore
need the greatest encouragement, and ought to be increased as much
as possible, that therefore spinning schools be set up in such places
and at such distances as the directors shall appoint, where whoever
will come to learn to spin shall be taught gratis, and to which all per-
sons that have not forty shillings a year estate shall be obliged to send
all their children, both male and female, that they have at home with
them, from six to fourteen years of age, and may have liberty to send
those also between four and six if they please, to be employed there in
spinning ten hours in the day when the days are so long, or as long as
it is light when they are shorter; provided always that no child shall
be obliged to go above two miles to any such school.

"That all children who are thus obliged to come to these schools shall
be paid for what they earn there in spinning, according to the ordinary rate paid to others, first deducting from each of them what they
have spoilt in tow or flax in their beginning to learn.

"That all in general who come there shall have wheels provided
them, and that they who are able to spin in Mr. Firmin's double wheel
shall, at their going away, have one of those wheels given them.

"That no wheel shall be used in any of those spinning schools but
what shall be turned with the foot and have the distaff placed in the
middle, so that, both the hands being at liberty, sometimes the one,
sometimes the other, may be used to draw the flax, the only way to
fit them for the double wheel, which they can never use unless each
hand can draw the flax with an equal facility.

"The use of this double wheel is of that great consequence to the
linen manufacture that nothing can contribute more to the advance-
ment of it than the bringing this wheel in fashion, they that can use it
being enabled thereby to earn very near double with the same labour,

and it deserving therefore by all ways possible to be encouraged. In order thereto we humbly propose---...

"*That at every summer assizes it may be lawful for any female inhabitant of each county respectively to come there and show her skill in spinning on the double wheel, and that she that shall there in one hour spin the most and best thread, to be judged of by the grand jury, shall have 10l. paid her upon the place by an officer to be appointed thereto by the directors, and moreover be recorded in court a mistress spinner and thereof have a certificate delivered to her in parchment, without fees, under the hands of the judge, the sheriff, the foreman of the jury, and such of the justices of the peace as will sign it, which shall entitle her and her husband, whenever she shall be married, to a freedom in any city, town, borough, or corporation in Ireland, to set up there what trade he or she shall think fit, with an exemption to the said husband during his life from serving on all juries and bearing any manner of office which he himself shall not be willing to undergo.*

"*And, to the end that no person by reason of poverty or distance from the place where the   assizes are held may be hindered from showing her skill upon the double wheel and may be somewhat considered for the charge in coming and bringing her wheel and flax, every one that comes and can spin so well on the double wheel as to be capable of a trial to be a mistress spinner shall be allowed twopence per mile from the place of her habitation to the place of the assizes, to be paid by the same officer to be appointed thereunto by the directors as aforesaid.*

"*That if any double-wheel spinner, during her following that way of living, shall by sickness or other calamity be disabled from getting a livelihood by spinning as she used to do, and be thereby reduced to the public relief, she shall have double the allowance that any other person in her circumstance hath or is wont to have.*"[19]

While the remainder of the text is historically interesting, it does not deal with the double wheel further.

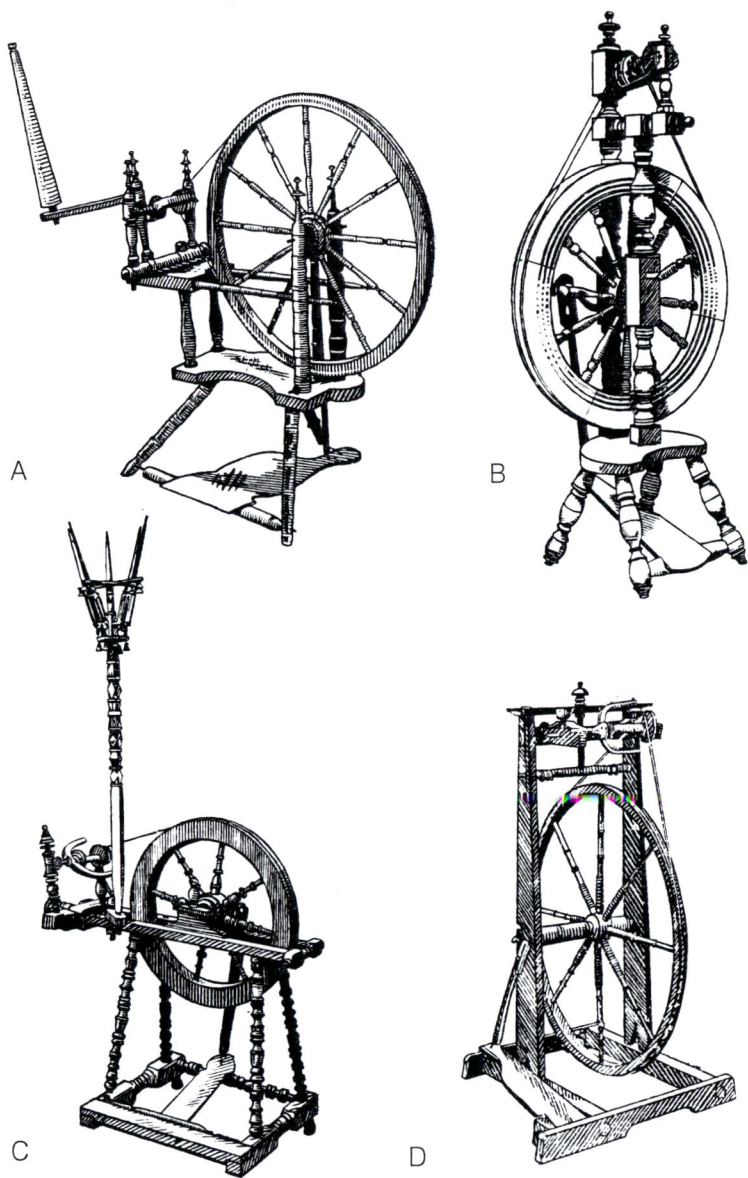

Wheels by country of origin.
(A) Norway (B) Germany (C) Tyrol (D) Austria

Chapter Two

Repairs and Restoration

It is better to wear out than to rust out.[1]

W hether a piece that has family ties, a special find, or just a working wheel that has a few problems, it is the nature of any mechanical tool to require maintenance on occasion. Often, there is little guarantee that a bargain wheel will actually be less expensive than a newer reproduction in the end. That said, knowing how to do any repairs required—yourself—not only saves a bundle, but insures that repairs are done as expected.

Whether a well loved wheel, or auction bargain, repairs are often necessary. In any case, a trusted shop-helper is a welcome asset.

The unique pleasure in using a restored wheel, lovingly built with simple hand tools, is difficult to describe. Part of this is that a spinning-wheel is a *personal* item, a treasured article with history. In restoring such an item one should not be surprised to sense a presence nearby, and perhaps, a whispered answer to the questions that arise when marvelling at the craftsmanship at hand.

Not every old wheel has the potential to be put back in service, though many do. The restorer has to weigh several aspects when considering the type of repair, or restoration, appropriate to the wheel. Sometimes conservation alone will be the best, and right choice. With this in mind, the following questions should be addressed before starting any restoration project:

—1. Is it possible to restore the piece without lessening its historical (or monetary) value?

—2. Can the function of the piece be restored and retain the *feel* of an antique?

—3. If the goal is: not to restore the function. What must be done to preserve the piece without destroying the evidences of time?

There is some feeling of obligation to put a good wheel back in service; however, the question of conservation versus restoration cannot be denied its place in the planning of such work. In beginning such a project, it helps to put oneself in the mind, and time, of the original builder. Materials: adhesives, leather, fasteners, and tools are drastically different today than those used at the turn of the 20th century. Go back another fifty years and another period of transition is found. As such, the requirements for restoring a factory made Canadian production wheel are quite different from a New England colonial period wheel. One may generally dispense of such concerns with a post 1940's wheel.

Assessing Required Repairs

Regardless of what level of treasure the reader has, the type of repairs a spinning-wheel may require are generally common to all periods. From making a replacement footman to putting a flyer back into working condition, all are within reach with a little time and patience.

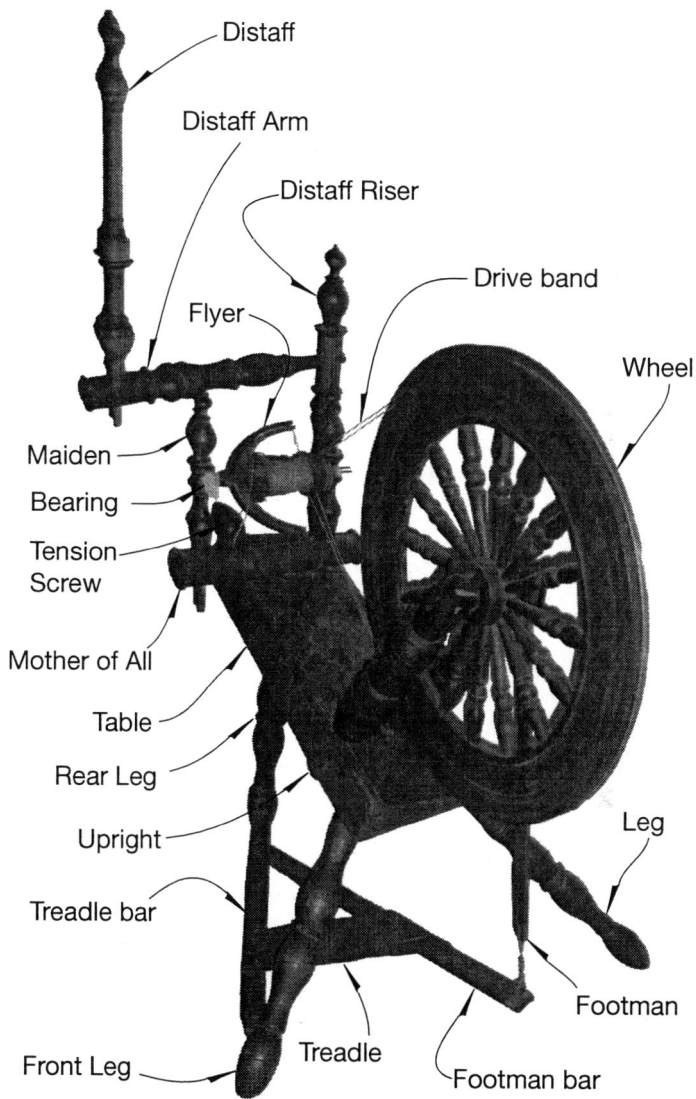

Typical parts of a Saxony style spinning wheel.

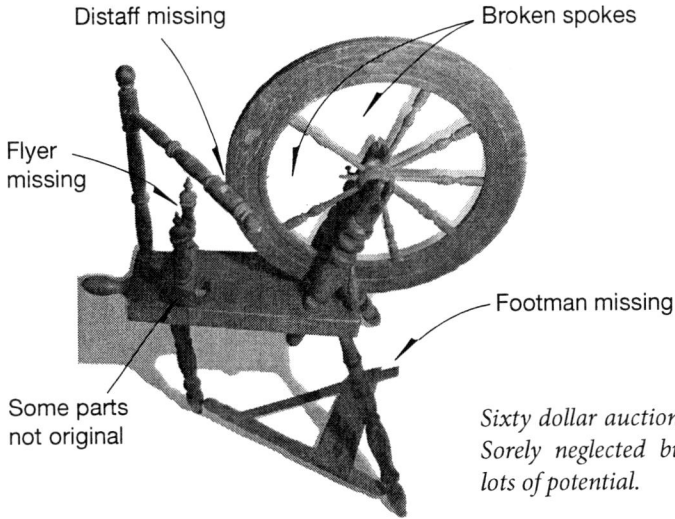

Distaff missing

Broken spokes

Flyer missing

Footman missing

Some parts not original

Sixty dollar auction wheel. Sorely neglected but with lots of potential.

Sometimes the task is as easy as re-assembling the parts in the correct order. The worst case situation often is: several parts are missing or broken beyond repair. It is quite common for the footman to be broken or missing; this is easily fixed with a hand drill and file, or rasp. For the bargain hunter that has purchased an old wheel missing a flyer, the stakes are considerably higher.

Just a few years ago, this would have necessitated finding a woodworker with suitable skills to fabricate a new assembly. Today, it is rather easy to find a replacement assembly using one of the various auction services. Buying a flyer assembly in this manner does involve a bit of risk; the sellers of such items often acquire their goods at bulk auctions, and rarely have sufficient knowledge of the features which the buyer will find important. The well-informed seller will usually provide a sketch of the important dimensions in the advertisement. For the handmade wheel, many variations are possible; this makes knowing the size of flyer you require essential.

When fixing broken flyers and wheels, repairs are most successfully done if there have not been previous attempts involving modern adhesives. The type of adhesive used will determine the extent of additional damage done. Rarely was any glue used in the building of these old wheels; nevertheless, on occasion some variety of animal based glue may be found. The modern term for these types of glue is *hide* glue; actually any combination of hide, blood, or bone may have been used.

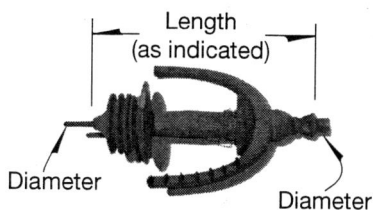

Minimum dimensions to ask an auctioneer for, when considering a used replacement flyer.

It is very discouraging for a wheel repairer to see a previous repair which has been done with modern glue. Complete removal of the substance is usually required. The wood beneath can be quite difficult to revitalize; the surrounding wood often softened or otherwise contaminated in the process.

Dealing with Old Woods

Perhaps one of the more challenging tasks for the restorer is achieving a good visual effect of any new parts added to the wheel. Matching the species of wood is just one of the aspects to consider when new parts must be made. Age darkening, accumulation of years of dust, and wax of various types, normal wear and tear, and the cellular breakdown that comes with age must somehow be added as well.

Creating the illusion of an age begins with proper selection of the wood used. When attempting to match old wood, the first consideration is the grain of the existing parts. Is it a close grained or tight grained wood? Often finding an exact match is not very realistic, the country of origin dictating the species of wood used.

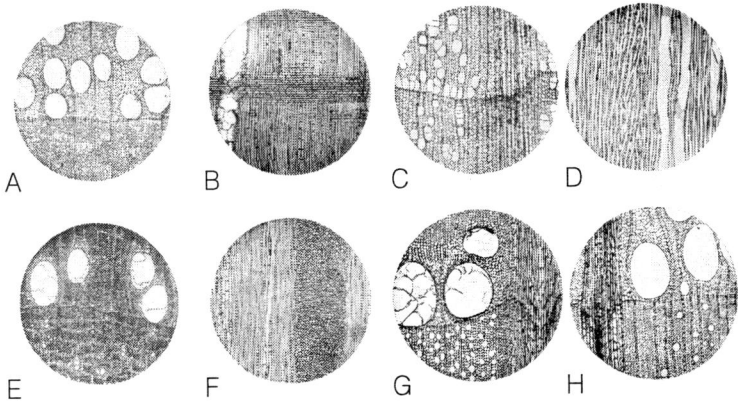

Fig. 2.1 ▸ A. *Black ash, cross section. B. Black walnut, radial section. C. Red alder, cross section. D. Red alder, tangential section. E. Shagbark hickory, cross section. F. White oak, tangential section. G. White oak, cross section. H. Red oak, cross section.*[2]

The next best choice is to find a close match. Sometimes beech will suit the grain of an old oak piece better than the oak that may be found. One must visualize how the grain will accept the chosen finish as well.

If it is possible to establish the geographic origin of the wheel, a review of the native trees can help narrow the possible wood types. From there, the nature of the grain and cell structure is established to narrow the search further.

Comparison of Hardwoods	
Large pores	Small pores
Ash	Alder, red
Chestnut	Beech
Elm	Cherry
Hickory	Cottonwood
Mahogany	Maple
Oak	Poplar
Walnut	Sycamore

Many methods of testing require an intimate knowledge of botany, and laboratory work, beyond the scope of most woodworkers. A quick examination of a thin slice under magnification can help narrow the field. A cross section slice, using a sharp knife or razor, and perpendicular to the vertical grain, is perhaps the most useful. Viewing the details is aided by 10x - 15x magnification; however, this is not always essential. Samples like those in Fig. 2.1 are available in several works, and provide a ready reference.

Powder Post Damage

The mother of all below shows an extreme case of a common affliction found in old wood, the minute holes left from an infestation of the Lyctus beetle. Sapwood will usually have the majority of the damage; this is the part the beetle finds the tastiest. Damage to the heartwood is also done by the maturing beetles as they emerge from the wood. Methods of seasoning hardwoods used in the pre-1900's included leaving the lumber in stacks to air dry, thus allowing the beetle a chance to multiply and burrow. The primary woods affected are: hickory, ash, and oak, common hardwoods used in spinning-wheels. Many other woods may also show signs of attack; black walnut, maple, and elm are found in this group.

One early method of stopping the damage was to saturate the wood in kerosene. Kerosene, when dried, not affecting application of shellac or varnish. Other methods included treatment with 1 part creosote and 3 parts naphtha, steaming the wood, or heating to 200° F in a dry kiln.[3]

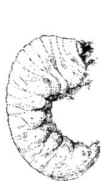

Preventing attack of new wood may be done by applying two coats of hot boiled linseed oil, during the peak season of the beetle between October and March. Many other insect species may be responsible for wood damage also. Most are insects that prey on the Lyctus, leaving much smaller emergence and exit holes in comparison.

The three stages of the "powder post" beetle. Scientific name Lyctus beetle

Planning the Project

Perhaps the most critical point of any restoration project is the manner in which the parts are disassembled for repairs. Many of the fits of most old wheels were done by hand, often with a pocketknife when it came to the fitting of small pegs. Non-permanent labeling of the parts should be done (at minimum) to keep ones sanity; putting these items back, in the order they were removed, can require good concentration.

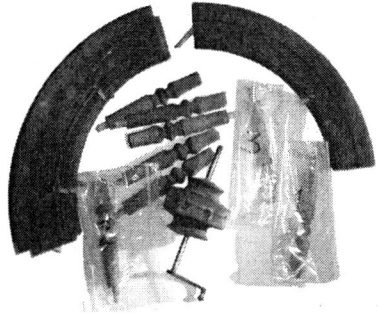

Some wheels may require complete disassembly. Any method of labelling should be easy to remove. This is not the time for masking tape.

In determining the method of labeling it pays to be a bit creative at times. The use of adhesive free tape for numbering is one method, another is sorting the parts into plastic sandwich bags. Sometimes an inconspicuous pencil mark, or a small scratch, in a location that will be hidden after re-assembly is the safest choice. Whatever manner is chosen, check then re-check that each piece has a matching hole identified before proceeding to the next part. Anyone that has taken something apart and later found that they have somehow acquired—extra—parts knows the reason for this pre-cautionary step.

Watch out for hidden nails and remove carefully when needed.

On the topic of extra parts, pay particular attention to small pieces, pegs and anything that looks out of place. Often these turn out to be small shims added to fix the fit between spokes and wheel, mother of all, or uprights. Save these and label where they came from for re-assembly.

Wheel Repairs

Major repairs to a wheel are always a last resort scenario. Often, older wheels are the most easily repaired; period methods of construction, as a rule, allow non-destructive disassembly. Taking the wheel apart is usually possible by removing pegs; newer wheels will likely be glued together.

While the joinery skills used in making these old wheels was remarkable in terms of simplicity and longevity, still an occasional bit of animal based glue may be encountered. Most of these old glues are soluble in water, and depending on the age by a little heat. Even though the joinery was remarkable, time will take its toll on the condition of wood. Sometimes these changes lead to the type of repairs shown in Fig. 2.4, as well as brittleness that can lead to breaks.

Should building a complete new wheel be required, the author's *Guide to Making Spinning Wheel Flyers and Wheels*, (Cooper Smith Publishing, Scotts Valley, 2009) describes the process in detail.

Old wheels usually exhibit incredible joinery. This wheel's condition was likely caused by using unseasoned lumber.

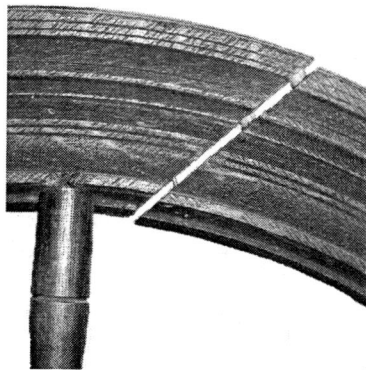

A common condition, often easily repaired. Pegs (seen in the gap) hold the segments together, usually without the aid of any glue. Carefully cleaning the surfaces, and using hide glue between can work. Clamping technique is key to success.

Fig. 2.2 ➤ Left: *The best case scenario for a break, with the grain of the wood. This allows for solid glue joints and is an easy fix.*

Fig. 2.3 ➤ Right: *A worst case scenario, double breaks across the grain. Even if the breaks are put back in order they will not hold without dowels.*

Broken Spokes

The examples in Fig. 2.2 and Fig. 2.3 show two types of common spoke breaks. The manner in which these may be repaired applies to most types of turnings, whether: spokes, legs, uprights, or the like.

The break in Fig. 2.2 is quite simple to repair. A bit of wood glue applied to the break is all that is required; the proper method consists of simply using enough glue to lightly cover the surface of one of the parts. This is next spread out across the area, working quickly. Following glue application, the two parts are clamped together. Where access allows, a rubber band works excellent as a clamp for small turnings. Whichever method of clamping is used, any excess glue that squeezes out should be wiped away before it dries.

The break in Fig. 2.3 is another matter, a hole must be drilled, and a dowel inserted between the two parts. This is necessary to provide sufficient strength after the join is made; otherwise, it shall likely break again.

A difficulty in drilling the holes for the dowel is the accurate matching required of the two sides. The most successful method to drill both on center is using a chuck to locate each part in the lathe. Still, one side or another is usually just a little off making the repair readily apparent.

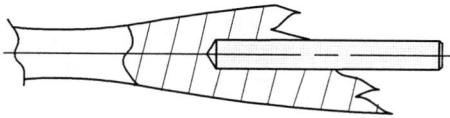

Step 1: Dowel is securely glued in one side.

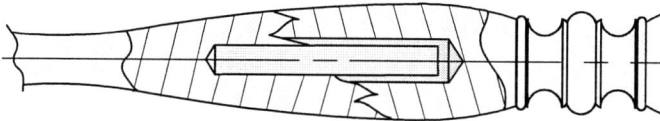

Step 2: A larger hole is drilled in the other side. The dowel is allowed to float in wood putty, keeping the two sides aligned to the natural edge of the break.

Inserting a dowel to strengthen a broken spoke. A loosely fit dowel, on one end, permits the join to match well. The area around the dowel is filled with a mixture of glue and fine sawdust.

One method of working around this is by drilling the hole in one side a bit oversize (about 1/64" bigger than the dowel). With the dowel glued tightly in one side of the break, a mixture of glue and wood dust is prepared for the other hole. The wood dust and glue mixture acts as flexible filler allowing the break to find itself; making a much more attractive repair which is still relatively sound.

For full replacement of a spoke, without disassembling the wheel, the split turn method is used.

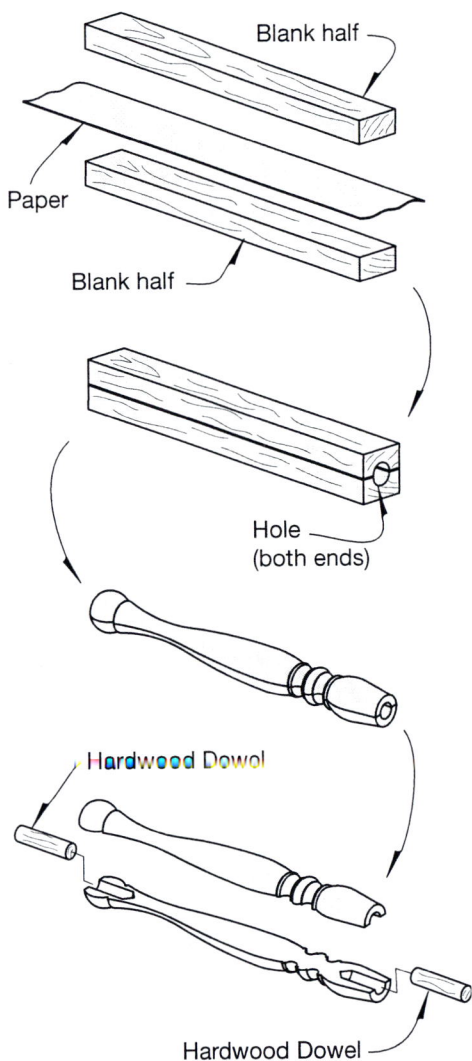

—1. *Paper is glued between two pieces of wood. Common white glue is fine; newsprint works well for the paper.*

<u>Note</u>: *Surfaces to be glued must be flat and well prepared.*

—2. *After the glue has had a chance to dry, a hole is drilled at each end sized for the dowel desired.*

—3. *Using the holes as turning centers, the spoke is turned and sanded.*

—4. *A plane iron and mallet are used to split the spoke in half again. The paper usually yields easily.*

After inserting one dowel in the wheel hub, and the other in the wheel rim, the spoke may be glued in place.

Split turning using a paper joint. A split turned spoke permits easy replacement in a fully assembled wheel.

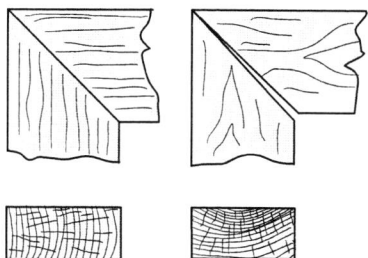

Grain direction and the cut of the lumber have much to do with the longevity of wheel joinery.

Left: quartersawn lumber

Right: flatsawn lumber

Reassembling the Wheel

Perhaps the most daunting repair is re-gluing a wheel which has fallen apart. This is a bit of a rarity, and—thankfully—the task often looks worse than it is. Common joinery for older wheels uses pegs to hold both wheel segments and spokes together. These are usually found to have been made by knife whittling, with each peg fitted to its respective hole. Removal may be accomplished by either pulling from the hole, or driving outward from the inside using a mallet.

The difficulty in this type of repair comes when the segments are re-assembled. Usually, the joinery between segments is incredibly accurate; however, (as in the

Fig. 2.4 ➤ *Filling the gaps created by time and humidity. Note the "peg method" of securing the spokes to the rim.*

case of the wheel in the following photos) even the craftsmen of old had a run-in with the effects of wood shrinkage on occasion. For such wheels the restorer must be a bit craftier to put things back in order.

Begin by removing any existing glue between the segments. A

short soak in vinegar should soften any hide glue, enough to permit scrapping it off.

Clean all the inside surfaces of the segments to be re-joined with some vinegar on a cloth; next, follow with a (very) light sanding. The idea is to clean the surface while not removing any wood. The segments are now positioned as they will be re-joined. An improvised clamp is useful to keep the parts together during initial positioning. The example shown in Fig. 2.6 is made from elastic cords (bungees) and clamping blocks made from closet rod, readily available at most home supplies. A quantity of small C-clamps make the job much easier; plan on two for each segment of the wheel.

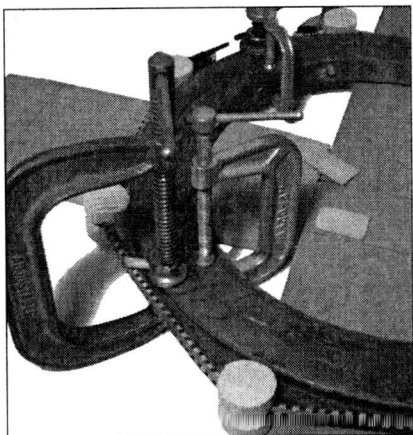

Fig. 2.5 ➤ *Clamping the wheel.*

The clamps are first used to lightly align the sides of each segment so that each lies in the same plane as the adjacent segment. At this point the diameter should be measured. A tape measure is adequate for this purpose; check the diameter in at least two opposing directions. Each measurement must match within a 1/16" of one another. If they do not match, re-adjust the position of the segments until they do. There should be no perceivable step felt on the outside rim of the wheel when a finger is ran across each join in the drive band groove. Each transition must fit perfectly, as when they were originally turned on the lathe.

Now it is time to warm the hide glue; this is done by placing the bottle in a pan of warm water for twenty minutes or so. The hide glue shall allow the time needed for the remainder of the assembly, common white glue will not.

Once the glue has warmed a bit and runs sufficiently, spread apart one of the joints (the elastic cord works nicely for this step). Now squeeze a dab of hide glue on the inside of the joint, spreading around until one side is covered, then continue to the next joint. When each join has been attended to quickly reposition the c-clamps, using one from the inner diameter (as shown in Fig. 2.5) and if necessary a second clamp from the outer diameter.

Fig. 2.6 ➤ *Holding the wheel segments in position. Check the diameter in at least three different locations quickly before the glue sets.*

This last step is very important; repeat the measurement of the outer diameter, as previously described, and re-check each join between segments as well. Adjust the parts if needed, and (if all looks good) let the glue set in a warm area for at least twenty four hours. Fourty eight hours is even better.

Once the glue has set, replace the spokes and pegs in the same location from which they were removed, and give the wheel a test spin. Re-truing wooden wheels works in much the way that truing bicycle wheel spokes is done. A small adjustment, this way and that, tempered with much patience and attention to detail.

Loose Fits

The least intrusive method of correcting loose fits, of legs and uprights, is shown in the photo at right. An alternate method for loose legs involves cutting a slit in the tenon with a hand saw; a small wedge is then inserted into this slit and driven, along with the leg, into the hole. While this method is not recommended for use on antiques, it is effective. Please do not use glue to keep the legs or uprights in place. The next owner will be grateful if you find another method instead.

A strip of hog skin and a mallet is a time honored fix for a loose leg tenon.

A loose mother of all is a different matter. Often a bit of play can be used to advantage during spinning; however, after time

The years of being nudged by a spinner's knee have taken their toll on this mother of all post. With extreme damage such as this, a turned sleeve may need to be fitted.

this movement may wear at the dowel that connects the mother of all to the tension post. Excessive play may be eliminated by the same manner as that used for the wheel uprights; by disassembling the parts and inserting a bit of hog skin leather. Hog skin is nice because of its thinness, making it possible to compress into small gaps.

Aligning the Wheel Posts / Uprights

Many old wheels will be found to already have some sort of shim material from a previous repair. Being a time honored method, wheels that have survived through the years—intact—are often found to have a bit of material wedged in the hole between the table and upright.

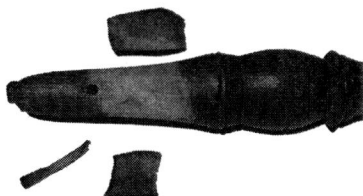

Shim material is used as alignment aid, and to keep the upright tight. A peg holds the upright snug in place.

For wheels that seem to slant away from the flyer, a well-placed bit of leather has a dramatic effect on wheel to flyer alignment. It is not enough to simply insert a shim in the hole and call it good; *where* the shim is placed makes all the difference.

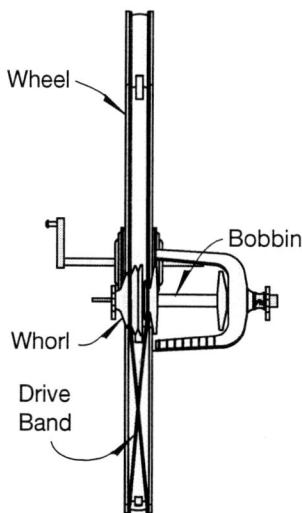

Wheel

Bobbin

Whorl

Drive Band

Sighting down the back to line up the wheel with the flyer bobbin and whorl.

Proper shim placement begins with first checking the position of the bobbin and whorl grooves in a line of sight with the wheel. Sometimes a little twist of the uprights, one in each hand, will bring the wheel in proper position.

If the wheel still does not line up well, moving any existing spacer material can help. If no spacer material is found: add some, then experiment with the positioning; forward of the upright, toward the back, until things start lining up. Sometimes the hole is just too large and the whole upright needs to be lifted out of the hole a bit. Continue in this way: back, forth,

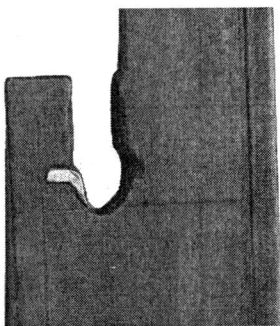

The forces of the wheel axle against the crank side upright lie mainly in the direction in which the bearing above has been placed. As the treadle drives the crank arm from top dead center (to about 20 degrees below) it is in the power stroke. Without a bearing, the upright often wears down and will eventually start to wobble a bit.

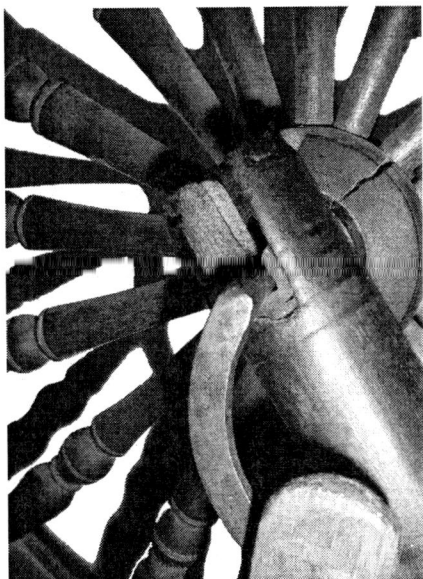

Dovetailed upright bearings show the maker's exceptional skill. Above: A wooden bearing with the grain running front to back Below: Bronze dovetail.

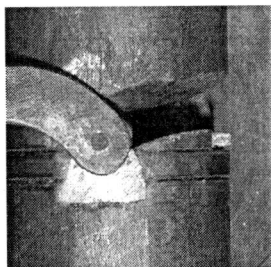

This upright had likely already worn some. A strip of thick leather has been formed in a "U" shape with another beneath for leveling.

up, or down. Each can significantly change the tilt of the wheel.

The Drive Band

Measuring the length of band needed is most easily done on the wheel. First loosen the tensioning screw and push it all the way forward. The band may now be installed by looping it around the front (facing the spindle side of the wheel) groove of the wheel, in a clockwise manner. It is helpful to tie the band off on the front maiden to keep it from rolling away if the wheel is rotated. Loop

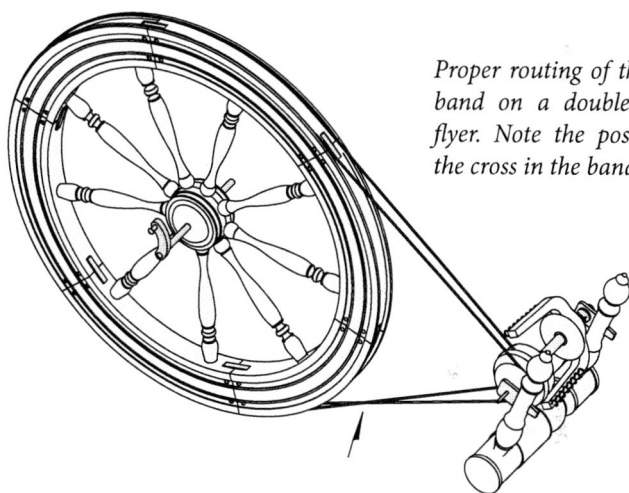

Proper routing of the drive band on a double driven flyer. Note the position of the cross in the band.

the band under and over the flyer whorl. Continue back to the rear groove of the wheel and under again. Finish by bringing the band under and over the bobbin groove, to connect with the end looped over the front groove of the wheel. The length of band, which is at the lowermost position and routed to the bobbin, should be above the length of band that is looped to the flyer whorl. This is to keep the band from rubbing where the two cross.

The ends of the band should now be joined by sewing together. Knots should be avoided when making a band join.

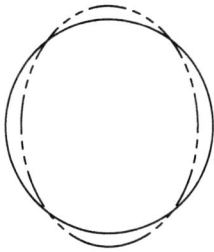

Above: A tight tension screw is often caused from warpage of the threaded portion.

Right: Sometimes it is just rubbing against the clearance hole itself. The latter is a much easier problem to correct.

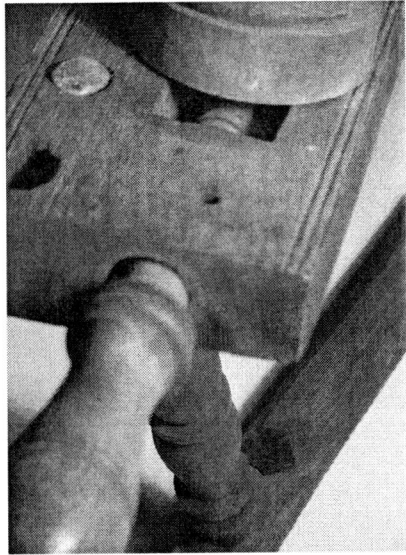

Tight Tensioner Screw

Admittedly, this can be the most dreaded of repairs for the restorer because it is often due to wood movement. If the wood used was not quite seasoned, the thread becomes an oval shape. If lucky, the thread may match a common threading tool; however, it is likely that carefully finding the high points, and sanding them down is required. A time consuming process it is, with no easy secret. Plan to devote the afternoon with a bit of 100 grit sandpaper and maybe a round file. Pencil marks in suspected high spots can help identify where the real problem lies. As the thread is turned the pencil lead will show the wear, and where to sand or file. Take your time and only remove as much as needed—no more. A little paste wax can help get things moving once the fits are close; another method is rubbing a bar of pure soap, such as Ivory, across the threads.

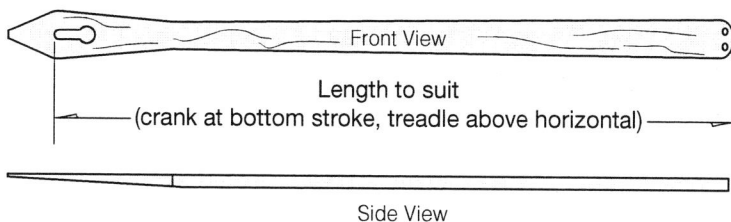

Front View

Length to suit
(crank at bottom stroke, treadle above horizontal)

Side View

Basic requirements for a footman. The holes at right are sized for a leather thong which will tie the footman to the treadle.

Making a Footman

A functional footman must have two features: adequate clearance through the stroke, and properly fitted length. Clearance begins with the large diameter in the key-slot; this should match the head size of the crank pin. The slot width must match the pin shank diameter.

A traditional wooden footman is usually tied to the treadle, using a length of leather thong. Some stretching occurs with use; expect to re-tie the knot occasionally.

Filing an angle to clear the crank arm, on the up stroke, is often required.

Left: Incorrect treadle angle. Evidence that the footman is not original.

Right: Correct footman angle at rest. A slight angle allows comfortable use.

It is important to keep the treadle plate position above horizontal at all times. The final length of the footman should be determined with the wheel completed, trimming material from the bottom as required.

Leather is sometimes used for treadle hinges. Left: A case of red decay made these straps break. Right: Repaired straps in place.
The use of nails to mount these straps is common practice and requires special care to replace.

Treadle Hinges

Few wheels have nails; nonetheless, sometimes they may be found holding a strap of leather that acts as a treadle hinge. In removing these to replace the leather straps, potential damage to the surrounding wood is of concern. Minimizing the damage, or controlling the type of damage, is often the best of available choices. Saving the nail is not always possible and sources for replacement can be elusive.

In the absence of a recycled original, Van Dyke's Restorers (source info in the Appendix) has a good selection to choose from. A reasonable substitute may also be made by hammering the head of a modern nail square, followed by artificially aging.

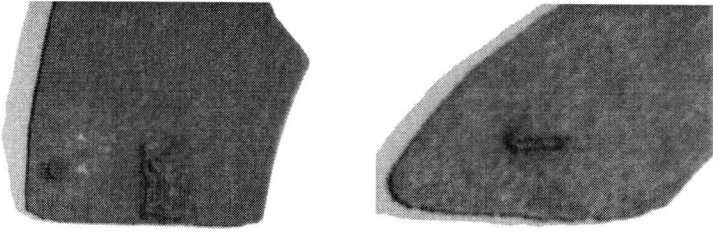

Fig. 2.7 ➤ *Left: The nail head side of the strap. These may be pulled out using gentle leverage. Right: The other side of the nail presents the problem. Removal without damaging the wood.*

Consider the nail in Fig. 2.7; the end of the nail has been pounded into the wood, making removal more difficult. Pressing the surrounding wood down a bit is usually required to allow access underneath the head. One method involves using a small, round-tipped punch to dent the wood on each side; just enough to permit grabbing the nail with needle nose pliers. The depressed wood may be steamed back into shape in the traditional manners for dents, such as using a hot iron placed on a damp cloth over the area. Another technique involves making a controlled cut around the nail with a sharp gouge (or knife), to gain access under the screw. The damage can then be covered by a plug, keeping the direction of grain the same as that of the piece to be repaired.

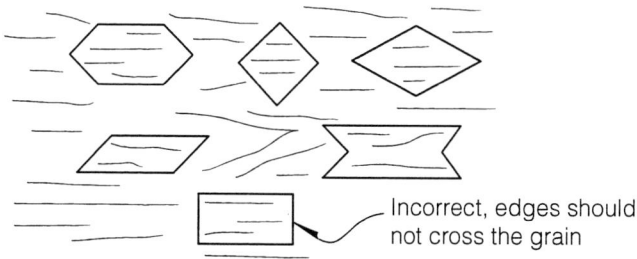

A few examples of good patching shapes. The hole should be a tight match for the patch, with the sides angling inward about 5 degrees.

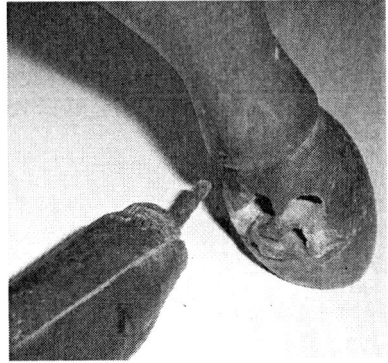

Left: It is common to find a treadle bar hole has worn down until the treadle rod will no longer stay put. Right: One previous owner's method of fixing the problem; continually drilling new holes as they wore out.

Many wheels have treadles which rotate about a metal rod inserted into a hole in two legs. At times it is necessary to drill new holes for these. The key to success is keeping the center-line of both holes true. The jig shown in Fig. 2.8 is made from two scrap blocks drilled to accept a *drill bushing,* and a length of metal rod that keeps the blocks parallel. Having drilled the first hole, a suitable rod is inserted through the bushing into the newly drilled hole. Thus aligned, the second hole may be drilled true to the first.

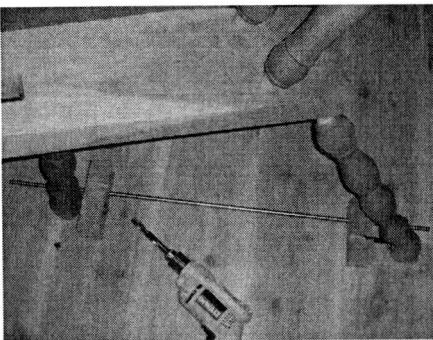

Fig. 2.8 ➤ *Using a drill jig to keep the treadle holes aligned.*

Old bobbins and whorls often split from end grain shrinkage. Patching with filler can make them usable again, keeping away yarn snags.

Patching Defects

There comes a time in any woodworking project when minor defects dictate the use of a patching material. The restorer is advised to steer clear of the various "ready made" concoctions that are found in the local hardware supply. Much better results may be found by mixing a bit of fine sawdust, using the wood to be matched, with an appropriate adhesive. The sawdust should be obtained from a fine-tooth hand saw, or band saw preferably. If using sanding dust, 220 grit sandpaper gives the size of wood particles which mix well with the glue.

A time-honored method is the use of (real) hide glue—that which is made up from the flakes—with the sawdust. A bit of powdered pigment may also be added if needed. In his 1995 book *Fixing and Avoiding Woodworking Mistakes*, Sandor Nagyszalanczy recommends adding a couple of drops of iodine, as a preservative,[4] to any leftover putty and enclosing in an airtight container to keep it from becoming rancid.

Some recipes of this type can be difficult to find, coming under the heading of trade secrets; nevertheless, the following collection have been found useful:

One recipe for wood cement

      — One part - fresh slaked lime
      — Two parts - rye flour
      — Enough linseed oil to make a putty
        (varnish may be used making the cement tougher)
      — Coloring if desired

Another

   — One ounce - brown rosin
   — One ounce - beeswax

Melt the rosin and beeswax in an iron pan; then add coloring if desired. Must be used hot as once it cools it can be very hard.

Crack filler

This one is good for large cracks, but must be allowed plenty of drying time. Stain may be applied over this for new work; add coloring if the existing area already has a finish applied.

   — One part - Cornstarch
   — One part - Wheat flour
   — One part - Japan Drier
   — One part - Linseed oil

Mix the flour and starch first. Add the Japan drier to the linseed oil, and add that to the flour and starch mixture.

When using any of these cements and fillers it is important to first apply any shellac, or varnish finish, desired to the surrounding area. The idea is to gauge the final color which the filler must match. A good idea also for oil finishes; however, extra care must be taken to keep the oil from permeating the area where the filler is to be used, lest it interfere with the filler having good adhesion.

For very minor cracks and scratches a cabinetmaker's wax may be made as follows:

   — One teaspoon - gum shellac
   — One teaspoon - pulverized rosin
   — One walnut sized chunk of beeswax

Place all three ingredients in a suitable container and melt over heat. Coloring may be added as needed. Use like sealing wax.

Using Modern Glues

Mixing a two-part epoxy with 220 grit sanding dust is one method useful for dark woods like walnut. A common white glue works better for lighter colored woods.

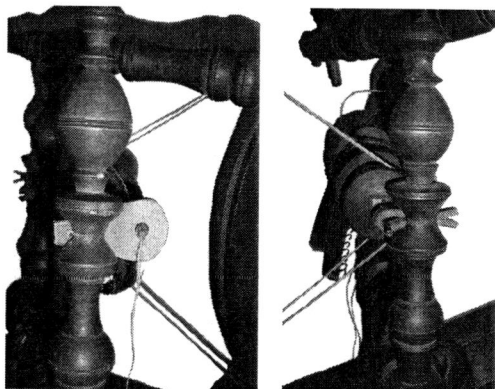

Left: Front maiden
Right: Rear maiden

Maiden Bearings

Maiden bearings come in a variety of designs. Upright wheels may have a simple bearing, like the one shown on page 48. Others use a folded strip of leather (above right) for the rear maiden, and a pierced band for the front. The maiden angles for this arrangement, are often different for front and rear; for wheels that are missing bearings completely, this can be a clue to the type of bearing style required for replacement. The method of retaining the leather may be a sliver of bone, or wood, placed through a hole in the two ends of the fold, or a wedge hammered in between.

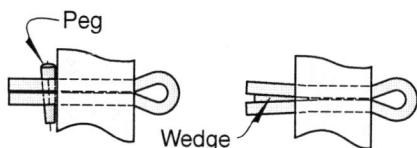

Common methods of retaining rear maiden bearings. A peg pierced thru, or a wedge between.

Leather Restoratives

The degree to which restoration is desired shall dictate the choices one makes in regards to old leather. Sometimes the choice will have already been made for you; even so, if the method required is a difficult one then it won't hurt to try a bit of neutral oil.

Many old bearings will be beyond repair; still, if it appears the leather is worth saving a number of methods may be tried. A cloth damped with lanolin is an excellent choice. Vaseline may also be used to wipe down the surface if it isn't far-gone. Oils such as: castor, rape (canola), olive, and tallow are good for softening leather. Rape oil and olive oil should be used in moderation, and only the best grades will do as there may be acidity from processing. While tallow was often mixed with neat's-foot oil for harness dressings, it is an unlikely choice in today's market. (Probably just as well as the odor can be a bit objectionable.) Fish oil is another option, and acid free mineral oil won't do any harm either, if the previous choices won't do.

Many recipes for leather restoratives include a medium for aiding penetration of the oil. Some indicate mixing the oil in alcohol or some other solvent. For most circumstances this practice should be avoided when revitalizing the thick leather found on spinning-wheels. Often, it is sufficient enough to warm the oil to aid penetration instead.

Soaking the leather in castor oil is probably the best of choices for leather that has hardened. Leave the oil on until it has had a chance to penetrate the pores of the leather, repeating the process until the leather has softened.

Most leathers which have not degraded considerably will benefit from a 1 to 1 mixture of castor oil and neat's-foot Oil. Some sources lean toward a 60-40 mixture so a little variance in the ratio should still provide the desired results. The two should be mixed well, and then be warmed prior to application.

For leather which has begun to flake, or is in generally bad shape, the following recipes have been found to give good results. The mixture should be rubbed in well; repeated applications given until an improvement in the condition is achieved.

One caution: following treatment, some means of evaporating the water should be undertaken. If left wet, thick leathers will mold, thus encouraging further damage to the leather. The idea is to get the oil in without leaving any water. A low wattage hair dryer is one option to aid evaporation. Direct sunlight is another but don't over do it; over exposure to sunlight also degrades old leather.

— 30 percent - anhydrous lanolin
— 12 percent - castor oil
— 5 percent - pure Japan wax
— 3 percent - powdered sodium stearate
— 50 percent - distilled water [5]

Another variation of this recipe uses neat's-foot oil in place of the castor oil, with slightly different amounts given.

— 25 percent - neat's-foot oil, pure, 20 deg C. cold test
— 17.5 percent - anhydrous lanolin
— 10 percent - pure Japan wax
— 2.5 percent - powdered sodium stearate
— 45 percent - distilled water

For either method, the sodium stearate and water are to be mixed separate. Heating the two together—gently—will help the stearate dissolve. The wax and oils may be melted together in a double boiler. The sodium stearate and water mixture is then added (in a thin stream) to the melted oil and quickly mixed in. Store in a sealed container to keep the mixture viscous.

For the restorer with a valuable preservation project, more targeted techniques are outlined in John Waterer's *A Guide to the Conservation and Restoration of objects made wholly or in part of Leather*, published by G. Bell & Sons, London, 1972. Many of the chemicals used in Mr. Waterer's methods should only be used with extreme caution and in a controlled situation.

Historical Methods of Tanning

The preparation of animal hides for tanning, before the middle of the 19th century, was (for the most part) different in respect to the materials used in the tanning process of the 20th century. For most restorations, this difference will likely be of little importance;

the use of petroleum products as lubricants for the leather, and other circumstances, having complicated the matter.

Wheels not previously subjected to petroleum based oils are becoming valuable auction commodities, providing the original leather is intact; the condition of which can be good, or not. In either case, it is helpful to know a bit about the historical methods of its manufacture.

Vegetable tanning is likely the oldest of methods, followed by the use of alum, with the chrome process being implemented around 1893 (though it had been known as early as 1858).[6]

One of the conditions that occur in vegetable tanned leather is known as *red decay*, shown in Fig. 2.7. Characterized by the crumbling of the top surface (exposing the inner leather), this of reddish color, and finally by its disintegration. Red decay occurs in leather that has been tanned using catechol tannages, these include: oak bark, the sumach *Pistacio lentiscus*, gambier, Australian mimosa bark, quebracho extract, and others. Acidity in lubricants, dyes, and such are contributing factors, as are the effects of sunlight.[7]

Flyer bearing of an upright wheel.

The method of tanning also varies depending on the intended use of the leather. Sole leather, the type used for maiden bearings having a drilled hole, is generally tanned by the vegetable process. Many old texts, which speak of the leather bearings of spinning-wheels, refer to the material as Ox-hide. Ox-hide and Boar

are especially suited for leather bearings as well as sole leather. Toward the end of the 19th century chromium became widely used to tan hides, and yielded a different quality of leather than vegetable tanning.

Leather flyer bearings of the bent over and pegged type, as well as other harness thickness leathers, might be made by any of the tanning methods in use at the time.

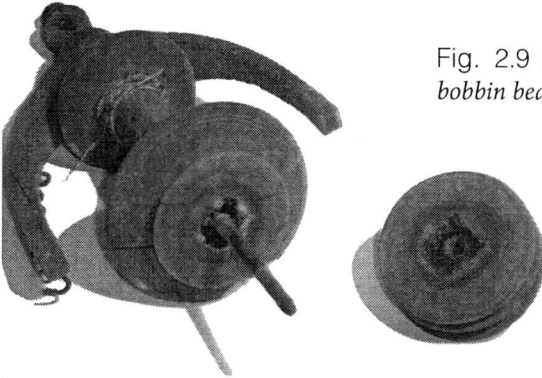

Fig. 2.9 ➤ *Mold on leather bobbin bearings.*

Bobbin Bearings

While not every old bobbin has bearings, those that do may have bearings made from leather. These were likely made of vegetable tanned leather, and efforts to revitalize them should be made with that in mind.

Leather mold may be found present upon removal of the whorl, as shown in Fig. 2.9. This can be removed by wiping down the leather with a soft cloth soaked in white vinegar. Another method is by a wiping with dilute alcohol.[8] Either denatured or rubbing alcohol may be used, mixed in equal portions of water. After wiping down, the leather should be left to dry in a warm, well ventilated area. Outdoors, in direct sunlight, is a good option. To protect against mold returning a good wax dressing should be applied once the leather is dry.

Removal of old whorls is generally in the direction shown. Left hand threads are opposite the commonly used modern bolt and nut.

Removing the Whorl

Whorls are close to flyers as the most common task when restoring an old wheel to working order. Sometimes, in the process of trying to remove the bobbin, the whorl (often already rusted up with gummed threads) is tightened more in the attempt. These efforts to un-thread the whorl, in a direction opposite of what is required, are a common mistake.

The flyer body should be held securely at the thickest part surrounding the flyer shaft, in a woodworker's vise to keep any pressure away from the flyer arms. With the flyer safely held, a strap clamp (like the one below) can be used to grip the whorl. By using leather for the strap band the whorl may be gripped nicely without chance of damaging the whorl grooves. Applying a bit of rust penetrant (such as Liquid Wrench) can make things go much easier if the whorl is stubborn. Be patient and allow the penetrant time to work before attempting removal.

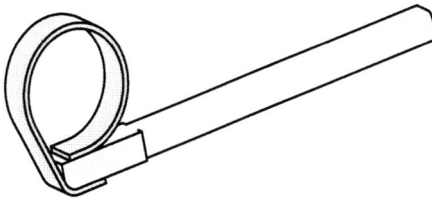

Sometimes a bit of leverage helps to remove a stubborn whorl. A homemade strap clamp fits the bill.

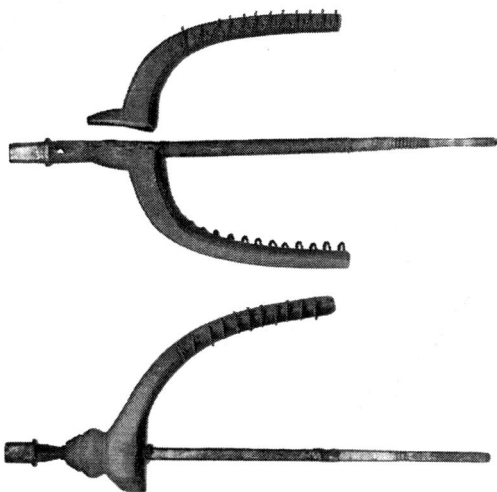

Two common types of flyer break

Above: Breaks down the center of the shaft are usually not successfully repaired for long.

Below: Breaks on only one arm have more surface area for glue bonds as well as room to add some metal reinforcement.

Flyer Breaks

Occasionally a flyer gets broken in the process of removing the bobbin. A slip of the hand, and one of the arms hitting the floor just right will do it. With a little luck this type of break may be glued back together; to survive until it is dropped once more, at which point further gluing becomes futile. When gluing such a break, the first time, it is important that the exposed wood of the break not be touched, or otherwise contaminated. Successful gluing requires that the wood fibers are clean of any oils if the join is to last.

Clamping such a break is the hard part. Providing there is an adequate shoulder on the flyer, rubber bands are usually the clamp of choice. Should there be enough material to screw the two pieces together as well, a small steel screw should be used. Brass screws of this size are not of sufficient strength for such a task. If after being repaired the arms appear uneven about the flyer shaft, a replacement flyer should be made and fitted to the old shaft.

When a break occurs further up on the arms, such as the break in Fig. 2.10, matching the halves back together can be even more of a problem, and clamping especially difficult. For these types of breaks a well-placed screw may be used (along with proper gluing) with some success. The repair below worked exceptionally well; however, it is somewhat advanced for most casual restorers. Still, a fine repair to attempt. If the repair is not successful the next step is replacement. After completion of any flyer repairs the balance should be checked and adjusted if necessary.

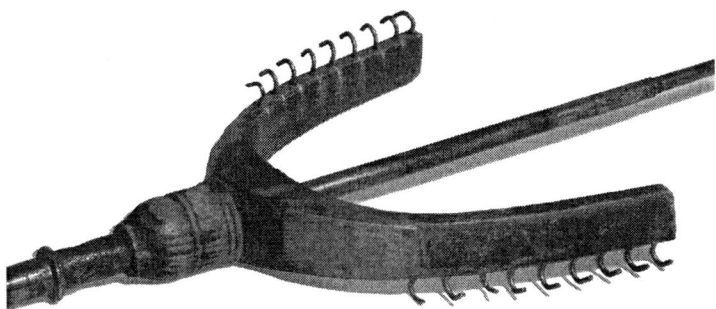

Fig. 2.10 ➤ *A sturdy repair using a thin metal plate. Headed pins, straddling the break, are inserted from the opposite side and extend through to the plate. By countersinking the holes in the plate, the pin may be hammered flush to form another head which is then ground flush.*

Detail of the opposite side.

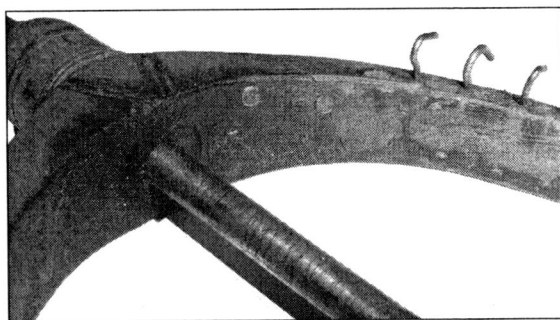

Worn Hooks

Flyer hooks are often bent lengths of heavy steel wire. It is normal for these to be worn through from the years of use, especially those used when spinning flax. These should be replaced using the same material and in like manner. The difficult part is the removal of the remaining bit of wire. One of the reasons is that the metal used for these wires is not particularly strong. Another, is they are often rusted through. To make removal more difficult, the inserted end may also be found flattened a bit on some wheels. With these, special care must be given to reduce tear out of the wood as the hook is removed. A set of vise-grips, or wire dykes, may be tried; nevertheless, pulling the wire out is still somewhat hit and miss.

For stubborn wires, just clipping them off flush with the wood, then filing down the remaining nub, is often the best solution. The area should be sanded smooth; leaving no part of the old wire exposed to interfere with spun yarn. A small hole is then drilled as close to the old wire as possible, the hole being a—very close—clearance fit with the new wire to be installed. The wire is bent to form a hook, and a small amount of two-part epoxy is mixed and inserted into the waiting hole with a toothpick. The wire is then inserted, making sure the bent end points the correct direction, and the epoxy is allowed to cure for the necessary time.

Regarding the material the wire is made from, likely some were made from fencing wire. In 1905 a special study was made by the

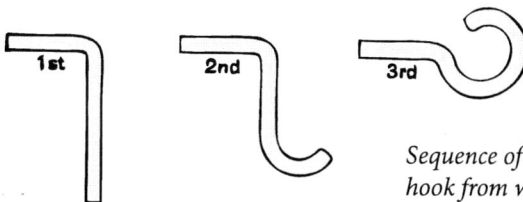

1st 2nd 3rd

Sequence of bending a new hook from wire.

USDA regarding the decline in quality of fence wire. The results of that study confirmed that fence wire (and flyer hooks one would suppose) made from wrought iron, was likely to last twenty years before rusting away. The new wire made from mild steel was prone to rusting away in a couple years. One interesting reason was considered at the time: "that the whole trouble lies in the greater amount of coal that is at present consumed, leading to an increase of corroding gases in the atmosphere."[9] Go figure.

His face with smoke was tand, and eies were bleard,
His head and beard with sout were ill bedight,
His cole-blacke hands did seeme to have ben seard
In smythes fire-spitting forge,...[10]

—Edmund Spenser, 1590

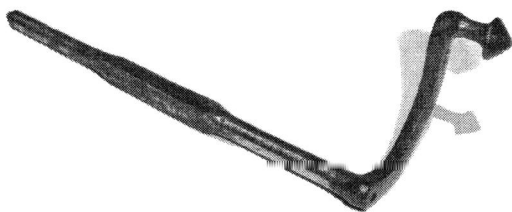

A hand-forged wheel axle and crank arm. Often made from wrought iron or mild steel, the shaft began as square stock; then beaten round in a process called "drawing out." The crank and pin were then welded on by heating the parts until the metal was nearly molten, and then joining them together.

Iron and Steel

When speaking of the different properties of steel the element *carbon* must be given its due. Iron nearly always contains some amount of carbon but it is the addition of more carbon which gives iron greater strength. Though at a cost to its natural toughness and workability.

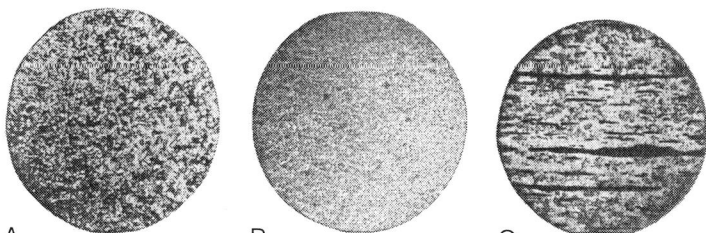

A   B   C

(A) Steel of 0.05 percent. Carbon rolled. (B) Steel of 0.50 percent. Carbon rolled. (C) Wrought iron showing slag deposits. [11]

Wrought iron of yesterday was a versatile material that was held in great esteem by the men who could work a forge and hammer. Once called "malleable iron" in Great Britain, wrought iron often bore deposits of slag (seen above).

By definition iron is: that "which is malleable at least in some one range of temperature," and being capable of hardening when suddenly cooled. The wrought iron of old was the perfect material for our spinning-wheel's axles and shafts, because of its natural toughness and workability.

Making the Wheel Axle and Flyer Shaft

A reasonable replica of a forged axle, or flyer shaft, is possible by using readily available stock shapes and perhaps the help of a machinist. While few home workshops today have such facilities for blacksmithing, it seems appropriate to look at how the axles of old wheels were made; if only for the sake of appreciation for the craftsman of yesterday.

Many of the wheel axles in use were made from a piece of round bar of malleable iron to begin with. The process of sizing the iron bar is called *drawing out*, done by heating, hammering, and shaping the bar in the following manner:

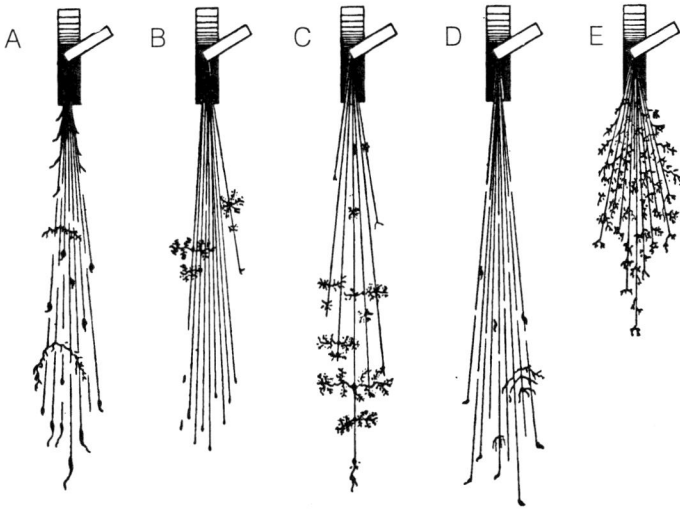

One method of determining the type of old iron or steel is to watch the sparks produced by contact of the metal with a clean cutting emery wheel. Surface speed of wheel should be around 7000 feet per minute.

(A) Wrought iron almost free of carbon. (B) Mild steel with a small amount of carbon. (C) Mild steel with 0.50 to 0.85 per cent of carbon. (D) Carbon tool steel. (E) High-speed steel with about 65 per cent carbon along with tungsten and chromium.

First, the bar is heated to as high a temperature as does not injure the quality of the steel. With the bar hot from the forge it is laid across the horn of the blacksmith's anvil, and given a blow with the hammer as shown below. Using the horn instead of the flat surface

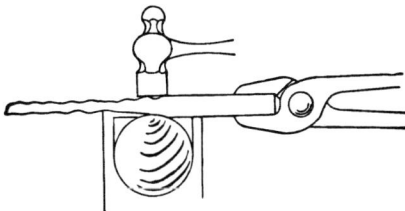

Drawing out. By hammering the bar on the anvil horn, the length increases more than the width.

of the anvil in this manner causes the bar to be lengthened with little spreading sideways.[12] (Another way to do this sort of lengthening is by using a *fuller* on either the horn or the flat surface).

As the bar is being lengthened, the displacement of metal is simultaneously reducing the cross section. Initially, the bar is squared up to the desired size (as for the ends of our axle) and then rounded up by forging the square into an octagonal shape. From the octagonal shape, the rounding up is finished in as few blows of the hammer as is possible.

With the ends of our axle finished to size, a little attention is given to the shape of the square section.

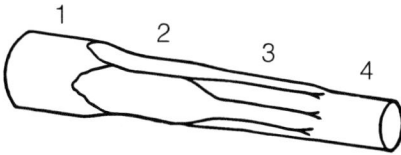

1) The original size of the bar. 2) Bar is sized square. 3) Square is forged to an octagonal shape. 4) Bar is finished round to size.

Possible shapes of the square portion of the finished shaft. Left in this manner the corners are likely to split the wheel hub when driven in.

Squaring up is done by striking the outer corner as shown. As the hammer strikes, a kind of sliding motion is given; forcing the protrusion back into the metal of the bar.

While a small deviation from a square shape won't be a problem, it is desirable to change a diamond shape into something closer to square. This will make fitting the shaft to our wheel hub easier and will be less likely to split the wood of the hub when it is driven in.

Heading the footman pin may be done in a number of ways; the manner of which depends on the tools at hand. The size of the pin used somewhat limits the available methods, as would the skill and experience of the smith. As with any type of manufacture, the choice of method used varies from the "one-off" method to a larger production scale.

Drawing down a bar, in a similar fashion to that already described, and then shaping the head is one method.

Another is: bending up a ring to fit a standard size bar, then welding the two together and finishing on a heading tool.

Upsetting a bar to form a head at one end is yet another method. First one end of the bar is heated alone until white hot, and then placed upon an anvil with the cooler end pointing up. With the hot end against the anvil, the cooler end is struck with a hammer, force being directed in a manner parallel to the anvil. The result is the beginning of a head at the hot end. Next the cool end is placed into a heading tool and driven in. In this manner, the head may be shaped as desired by hammering.

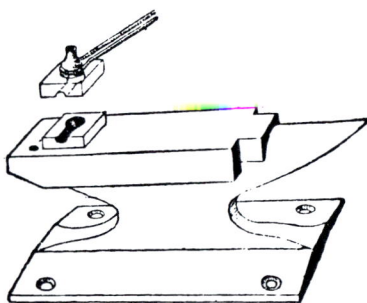

Swaging block and anvil.

Wheel makers doing considerable business might be inclined to make a die for shaping the hot iron into a ready made pin with head. A variety of swaging blocks may be used as well. The actual process depends greatly on which types of tools are to be used.

The remainder of the work needs little description, save for the obvious; that the three parts: axle, footman pin, and crank arm must now be welded together. The small size of the parts requires extra care at this step; skill and experience accounting for the excellent welding on most old crank arms. Perpetuating once again the "mysteries" of the wheel-maker's craft.

Cutting metal on a foot powered lathe using the "graver".

They begin to work firſt with the ſharp point of a *Graver*, laying the Blade of it firm upon the *Reſt*, and directing the point to the Work, and lay Circles upon it cloſe to one another, till they have wrought it pretty true : Then with one of the broad Edges of the *Graver* they ſmoothen down what the Point left...[13]

—Joseph Moxon, 1703

Early Metal Turning

Until the introduction of steam powered lathes in the latter part of the 19th century, many of the tools used for metal turning had not changed in several centuries. Perhaps the finest early instruction manual we have, for working metal, was written in the year 1100; attributed to a Benedictine monk known as Theophilus Presbyter. In John G. Hawthorne and Cyril Stanley Smith's translation of the Latin text, we see an engraving tool[14] pictured which is identical

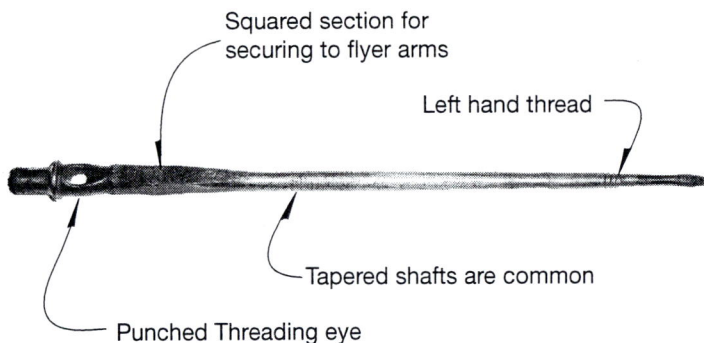

Squared section for
securing to flyer arms

Left hand thread

Tapered shafts are common

Punched Threading eye

to those referred to in nearly all turning manuals of the 18th and 19th centuries. Called the *Graver* since the time of Theophilus, its use for lathe work is perhaps best described by Holtzapffel in 1879. Moxon's description (previous page) of the Graver's use will explain those mysterious ridges often found on old flyer shafts.

Cleaning the Flyer Shaft

Cleaning of the flyer shaft is a very important task; especially, if the wheel is to be put back into service. Many novice spinners give up on learning simply because: the bobbin does not turn freely on the flyer shaft of their wheel. Unfortunately, this frequently occurs on modern mass-produced wheels, from poor quality control. One of the reasons for owning an antique is the craftsmanship of the fits between flyer, bobbin and whorls. This mastery of mechanics not often seen in products of today.

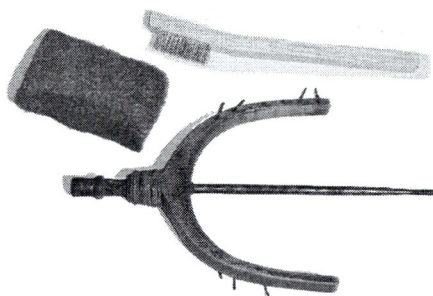

A wire brush and steel wool are used to clean the years of various oils from the flyer shaft.

Proper cleaning often begins with removing a bit of rust. Several modern compounds may be used, but their toxicity is an unnecessary hazard. The following method has been used for centuries, and is quite effective: "To take rust out of steel place the article in a bowl containing kerosene oil, or wrap the steel up in a soft cloth well saturated with kerosene ; let it remain 24 hours or longer; then scour the rusty spots with brick-dust. If badly rusted; use salt wet with hot vinegar; after scouring, rinse every particle of dust or salt off with boiling water; dry thoroughly; then polish off with a clean flannel cloth and a little sweet [olive] oil."[14]

Rust Preventatives-

Method 1. Melt together: 3 parts lard and 1 part powdered resin. Apply with a brush.

Method 2. Heat the metal and dip in linseed oil. The item may be blackened also by holding in a flame after dipping.

Method 3. Vaseline.

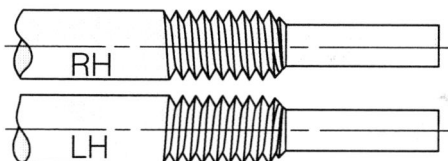

Top: Right hand thread. Bottom: Left hand thread.

Flyer Shaft Threads

On the occasion that a new whorl must be made, one cannot simply go to the local hardware store and expect to find matching nuts for the flyer shaft. First, there is that left-hand thing, and second, any wheel made before 1860 likely has a unique thread form. Some may look at the thread that remains, and determine that it is a 1/4-20. Perhaps close, but likely not quite the same.

A multitude of tools were used to cut threads during the reign of the spinning-wheel. Chasers might have been used if the threads were cut on the lathe. The left-handed thread on old flyer shafts would seem to indicate this, though left-handed dies were also available. Taps and dies appear in very early manuals looking much the same as those today. The difference in threads made then, and those made today lies mainly in the standardized forms.

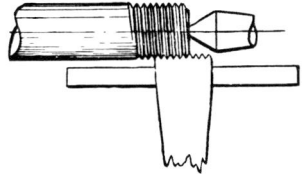

"Chasing" a thread. A left-handed thread is the easiest cut in this manner.

One common practice at the turn of the 19th century was to make a tap by filing a steel screw square, using the filed corners to cut the thread. The village smith or mechanic was also likely to have an oversize tap on hand, which may have found its way into use on a flyer shaft. These oversize taps and dies were designed to be used on standard, rolled bar stock; this was supplied 1/64" to 1/32" over the designated fractional size (for instance: a standard 1/4" rolled bar might actually measure 17/64"). Judging from an

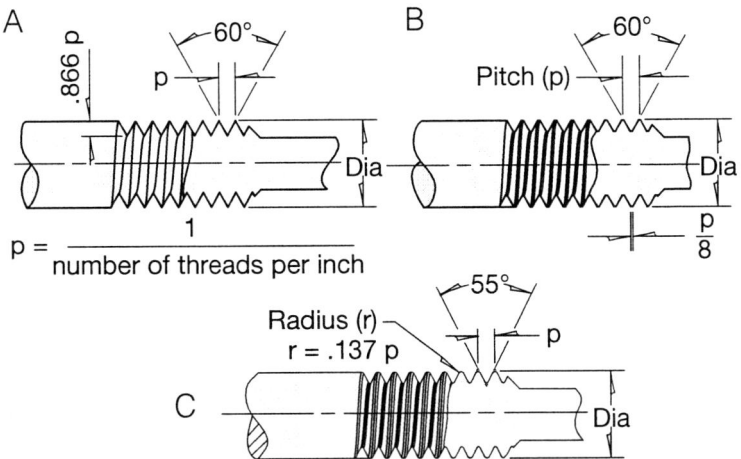

A

.866 p

$$p = \frac{1}{\text{number of threads per inch}}$$

B

Pitch (p)

$$\frac{p}{8}$$

Radius (r)
r = .137 p

C

Possible thread forms for old flyer shafts. A. 60 degree V-thread. B. US-Standard designed to replace the V-Thread C. Whitworth thread (Britain).

Sizes of Tap Drills - V Thread		
Diameter Tap (Inch)	Threads per inch (TPI)	Tap drill size
1/4	18	No. 17
1/4	20	No. 14
1/4	24	No. 9
9/32	16	No. 10
9/32	18	13/64 in.
9/32	20	No. 3
5/16	16	No. 1
5/16	18	15/64 in.

Sizes of Tap Drills -A.S.M.E. Std. Machine Screws (Proposed 1907)			
No	Outside Dia. - TPI	Root Dia	Tap drill size
14	.242-24	.1807-.1879	.1935
16	.268-22	.2013-.2090	.213
18	.294-20	.2208-.2290	.234

Sizes of Tap Drills -U.S. Standard Thread (Seller's thread)		
Diameter Tap Inch	Threads per inch	Tap drill size
1/4	20	No. 11
5/16	18	D

Sizes of Tap Drills -Whitworth Thread		
Diameter Tap Inch	Threads per inch	Tap drill size
1/4	20	No. 7 (.201)
5/16	18	.250 - .257

Sizes of Tap Drills -International Standard				
Mm	Inches	Root Dia	Pitch mm	TPI
6	.236	.181	1.00	25.4
7	.276	.220	1.00	25.4
8	.315	.246	1.25	20.3

TABLE 2-1 ▶ Tap drill sizes from the *Morse Twist Drill and Machine Co. Catalog*, 1913, and other sources.

early tool catalog,[16] a large majority of the tap and die sets were furnished 1/32" oversize of the nominal designation. A primitive *screw plate* also found use early on; as well as taps which tapered to allow finding a size that would work. In addition, the unpredictable nature of these thread-forms created a need for adjustment in the dies as well; further complicating things for the wheel restorer.

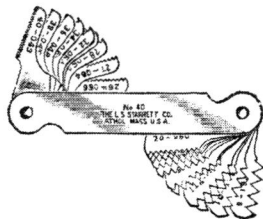

Thread pitch gages may be found for Whitworth, as well as the American Standard.

While a form of the V-thread likely already existed in these early threading tools, real standardization did not occur until 1841. Joseph Whitworth, of Great Britain, began the revolution in threads. William Sellers first proposed a standard for American threads in 1864, at the Franklin Institute. The British standard has been known as Whitworth ever since; the American thread form became known as the Sellers (or Franklin Institute) thread initially, later to be known as the United States Standard thread.

Wheels made in Europe are likely to have a different thread form than those made in the United States; requiring a bit of detective work (and some luck) when trying to make new whorls for old flyer shafts. Even for wheels made later than 1861. Such standards take time to be used widespread; the old tools still finding use well up to the beginning of the 20th century.

The second step in attempting to identify an old thread form is: finding the pitch of the thread. Pitch is the number of crests in a given distance; this may be in inches or millimeters. The next step is: to measure the thread diameters: root, crest, and (if possible) the pitch diameter. Measurement of the whorl nut itself may provide some clues as well, as the tap drill size varies also.

Accelerating Heads

So many types of accelerating heads were made as to require a book of their own. The style at right was produced in mass quantities by several makers, and represents the most commonly found example. At first, repairs to these look daunting; actually the repairs are usually of a minor nature.

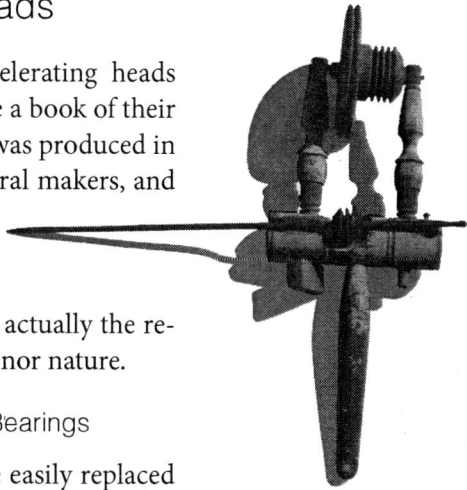

Replacing Corn Husk Bearings

Corn husk bearings are easily replaced using tamale husks from any grocery. The trick is to soak them until they become pliable enough to allow being braided without cracking. Once braided the ends are tied off with a length of thread. After allowed to thoroughly dry, they are folded over, inserted, and then tied off in the manner shown in Fig. 2.11.

For the purist, it is worth noting that different varieties of corn have husk material which is more abrasive than others. With much of the crops today being genetically engineered, a little experimentation may be necessary to find the right match.

Fig. 2.11 ➤ *Braided corn husk bearing. Left: front view, Right: rear view. Notice how the corn husk on the right is tied together.*

Missing Adjuster Nut or Top Bearing

These are an easy project for even an amateur woodworker; drawings are provided on the following pages should no other examples be available to work from.

Pulley Crack or Split

Often these cracks are from (natural) end grain splitting; filling is as previously described with one of the crack fillers.

Likely the most challenging of repairs is the replacement of one of the threaded uprights. While wood threaders are found from specialty wood supplies, the size of the thread commonly

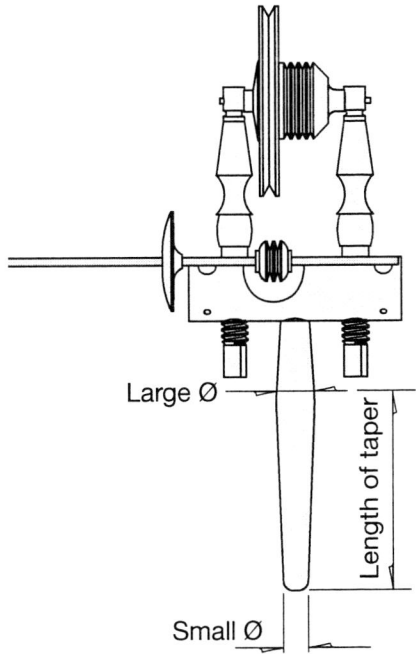

$$\text{Taper per foot} = \frac{\text{Large } \emptyset - \text{Small } \emptyset}{\text{Length of Taper}} \times 12$$

Measuring the taper, whether external or internal, is done by finding the diameter at each end and the length between.

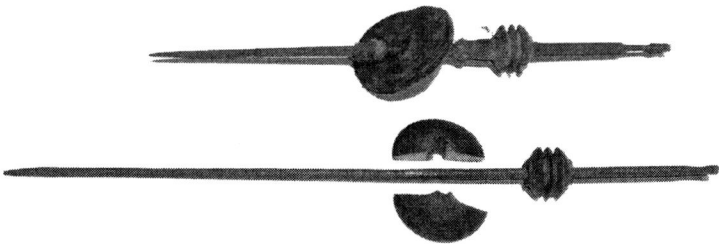

Yarn stops are sometimes found made from leather (above), an easy replacement for the original wooden ones (below).

used on these may not be available. For these special thread sizes—often a 5/8 inch diameter—a restorer will likely have to resort to making the tool themselves. The *Montgomery Ward Catalogue of 1895* shows these tools (they call a "wood screw cutter") in thread sizes of ¼, ⅜, ½, ⅝, ¾, 1 inch and so on, up to 2 inches. Unfortunately today the selection is not so varied.

While several books offer a look at how threading tools for wood may be made, the information found in *Fine Woodworking on Hand Tools* (Newtown, Connecticut: The Taunton Press, 1988), pages 42-48, gives an extremely complete account. Both the making of external and internal threading tools are covered.

Large Pulley
Intermediate Pulley
Pulley Shaft
Accelerator Pulley Assembly
Top Bearing
Maiden
Spindle Pulley
Yarn Stop
Spindle
Mother of All
Adjuster Nut
Mount

Fabricated components of the "Amos Minor" style accelerator head.

Detailed drawings for other parts of the *Great Wheel* may be found in *Foxfire 2*, edited by Eliot Wigginton, 1973. A particularly useful book for anyone interested in learning more of the craft.

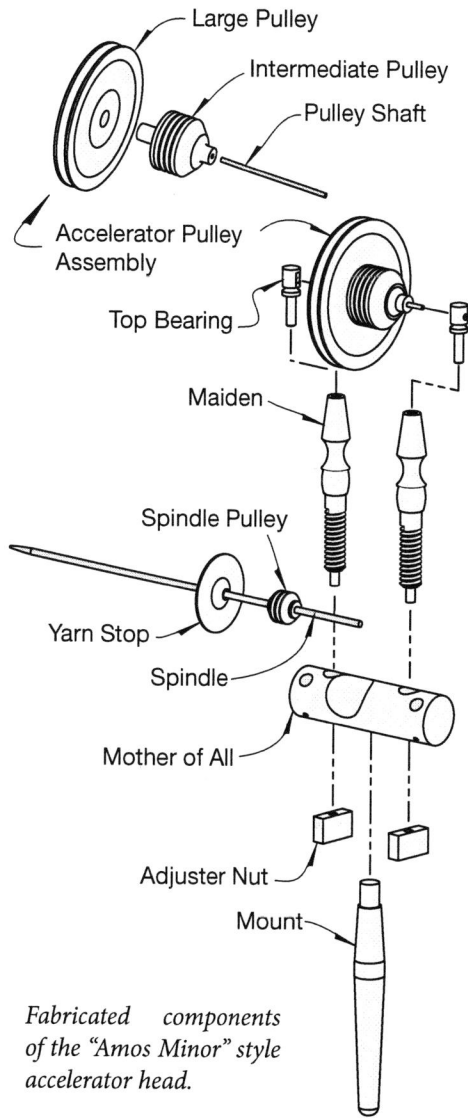

Top Bearing
Matl: Hardwood

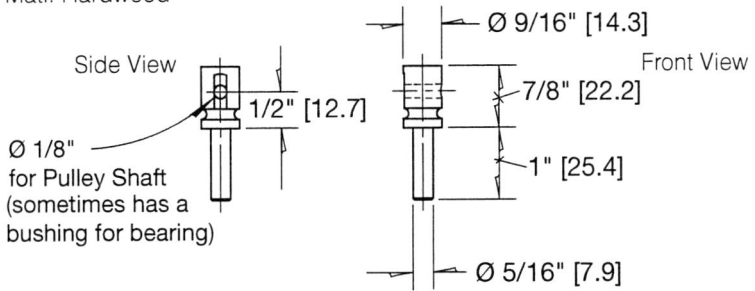

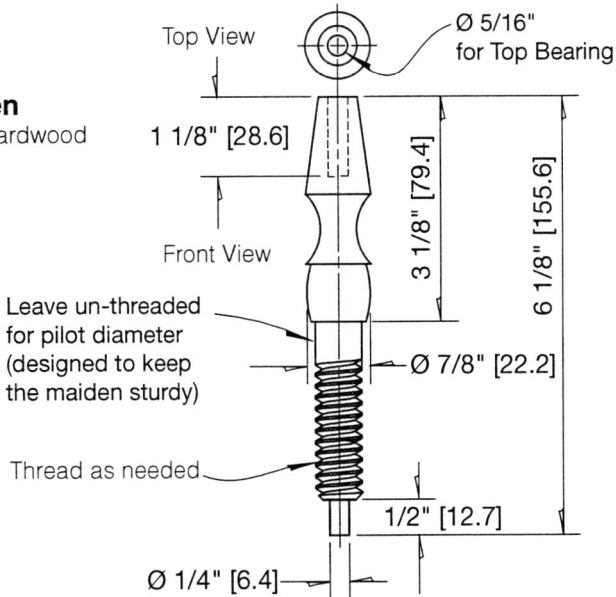

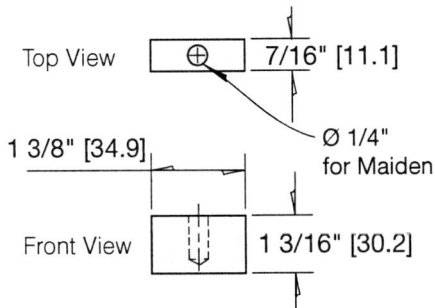

Side View

Ø 1/8"
for Pulley Shaft
(sometimes has a
bushing for bearing)

1/2" [12.7]

Ø 9/16" [14.3]

Front View

7/8" [22.2]

1" [25.4]

Ø 5/16" [7.9]

Top View

Ø 5/16"
for Top Bearing

Maiden
Matl: Hardwood

1 1/8" [28.6]

Front View

3 1/8" [79.4]

6 1/8" [155.6]

Leave un-threaded
for pilot diameter
(designed to keep
the maiden sturdy)

Ø 7/8" [22.2]

Thread as needed

1/2" [12.7]

Ø 1/4" [6.4]

Adjuster Nut
Matl: Hardwood

Top View

7/16" [11.1]

Ø 1/4"
for Maiden

1 3/8" [34.9]

Front View

1 3/16" [30.2]

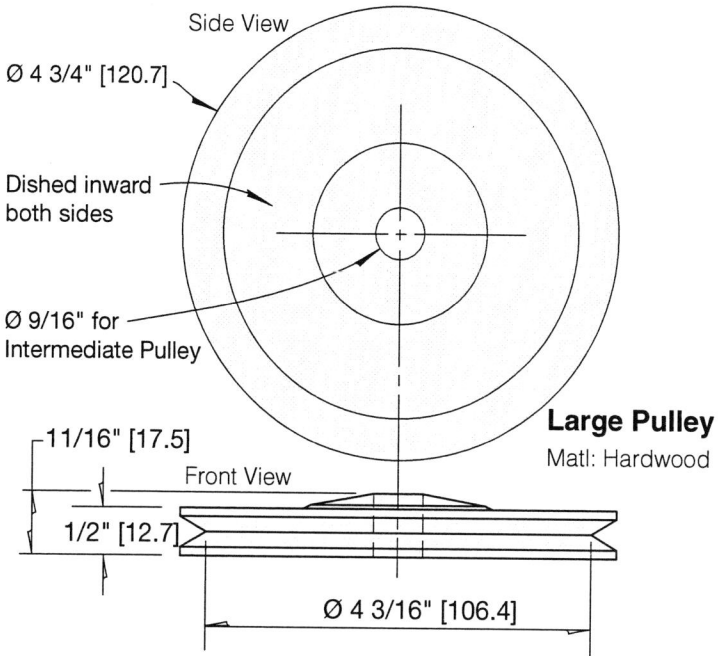

Side View

Ø 4 3/4" [120.7]

Dished inward both sides

Ø 9/16" for Intermediate Pulley

Large Pulley
Matl: Hardwood

11/16" [17.5]

Front View

1/2" [12.7]

Ø 4 3/16" [106.4]

Ø 9/16" [14.3]

Pulley Shaft
Matl: Mild Steel

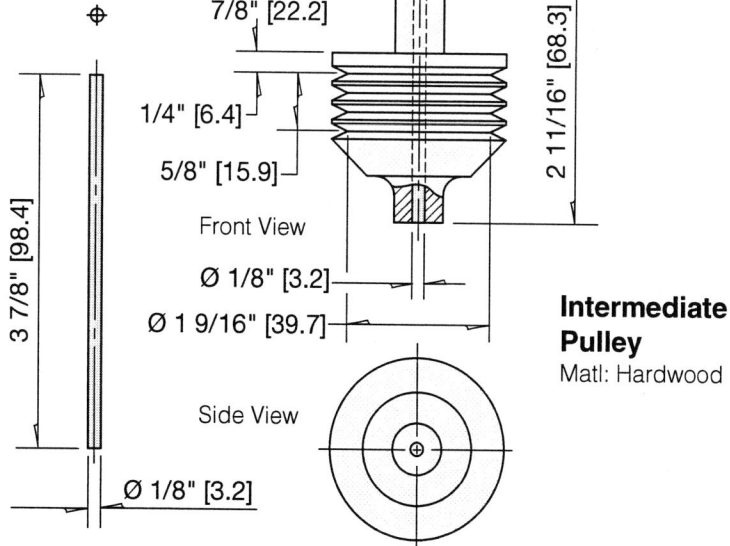

7/8" [22.2]

2 11/16" [68.3]

1/4" [6.4]

5/8" [15.9]

Front View

3 7/8" [98.4]

Ø 1/8" [3.2]

Ø 1 9/16" [39.7]

Intermediate Pulley
Matl: Hardwood

Side View

Ø 1/8" [3.2]

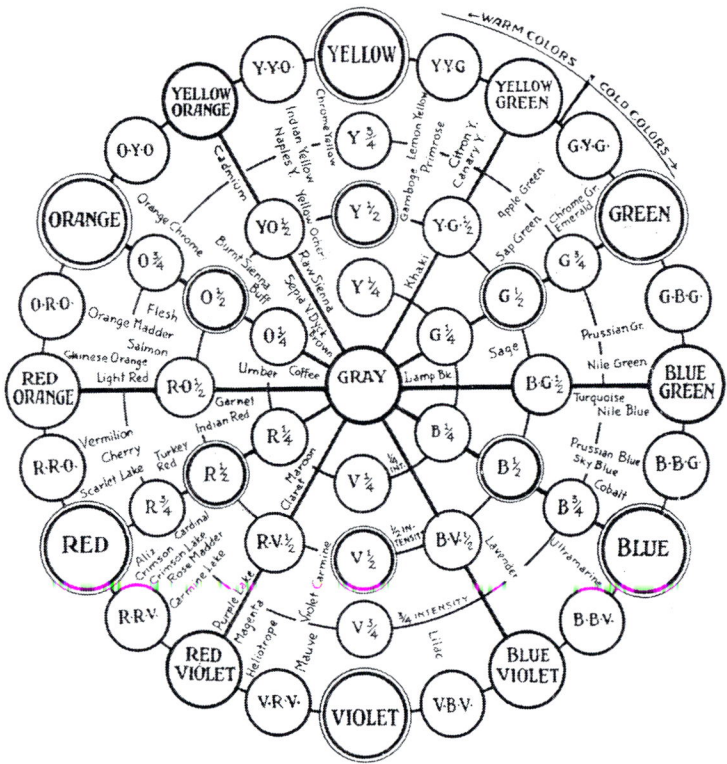

Color charts are useful when shades are "almost" right but not quite. The upper left quadrant of this chart is especially useful to the woodworker.

Chapter Three

Finishes

The "Antique" effect is produced by using a light filler colored with burnt umber, the amount of umber in the filler determining the color.[1]

Restoring old wheels differs somewhat from ordinary furniture restoration in that fewer finishes may be expected. Still, the basics begin with performing a solvent test on a finish that is not easily identified.

Assuming the finish is truly old, not necessarily original, two possibilities may be ruled out by testing a small, inconspicuous area with solvent. A bit of denatured alcohol on a rag is used to check for shellac; lacquer thinner is used in the same manner to check for lacquer. Let the solvent soak in for a moment, then rub the area with a rag. If neither denatured alcohol nor lacquer thinner dissolve the finish, it may be a varnish. If varnish is suspected leaving it alone may be the best choice at hand.

Time honored finishes: easy to use and difficult to mess up. Turpentine and vinegar help with cleaning. Linseed oil: (A) boiled, (B) raw, (C) polymerized (da kine). Paste wax (D) and an ultra-fine synthetic pad work wonders.

Cleaning

A bit of cleaning to remove any waxes present is desired before applying new finishes. Though it may seem too simple, a solution of environmentally friendly dish soap (castile soap is also good) and warm water may be the answer in many cases. Careful not to soak the wood; too much exposure to water will raise the grain, making the piece feel rough. Sanding is not a desirable thing when working with antiques, and should be avoided if possible.

The dark stains beneath the axle are often from tallow, a common lubricant before the age of petroleum oils. This adds character and value to the piece and is best left alone when cleaning.

For stubborn cleaning jobs: 3 tablespoons of boiled linseed oil, and 1 tablespoon of turpentine, mixed in a quart of mildly hot water[2] will do the trick. (This 3 to 1 ratio re-appears shortly and may be remembered as a "rule of thumb".) Use a soft cloth to clean the area then wipe down using a dry cloth.

Oil Finishing

Renewing an oil finish is practically impossible to mess up—perhaps with the exception of Tung oil. As with any substance, selecting high-grade products can improve the end result. The boiled linseed oil sold for household paint use can yield a disappointing finish for an antique. Do a little shopping and get the best quality you can. Raw linseed oil is usually of better quality and may be found in artist shops; this may be used if a drier is added, such as turpentine. A ratio of 3 parts oil to 1 part turpentine has been found to be adequate.[3] (There it is again.)

Before applying an oil finish, such as linseed, penetration is aided if the oil is first warmed up a bit. Any suitable vessel, deep enough to stand the can of oil in, may be filled with hot water from the tap.

For linseed oil finishes: initial application begins with the raw linseed oil and turpentine mixture. Leave the oil to warm 10 or 15 minutes (in that pan of water), before beginning application. Then use a brush, and don't get carried away. Turnings should be oiled by working around the part, this usually is across the grain, followed by brushing lengthwise with the grain. After applying oil to an area let it soak in a bit; then wipe down with a soft cloth and buff.

Allow the first application of oil, and any grain filling, at least a day to dry—after initial wipe down and buff—in warm weather, two or more days in cold weather. Next, three or more coats of oil should be applied using boiled linseed oil. (The raw linseed was for the initial coat only.) Give each coat ample time to cure before adding another, and buff after each coating. This process may be hastened dramatically by the use of polymerized linseed oil if it is available.

Priming the Wood

For unfinished wood, dry and freshly sanded, end grain on turnings may tend to darken more than desired. Further darkening may be reduced by sealing the end grain using filler, or other barrier, to slow penetration of the linseed oil. Colored pigment may also be added to the recipe for crack filler (page 44) if a different shade is desired. When using any paste filler mixture it should be wiped off with a rough cloth; once it dries enough to be fairly sticky. Waiting too long to remove the filler can result in more effort required to remove it than necessary. A mistake likely not repeated.

A thin coating of shellac may, alternately, be used on top of a first coat of oil; acting as a barrier against further darkening by subsequent coats of oil. Thinning a little paste filler with spar varnish is another method. Adding a bit of Japan drier is recommended to speed up the drying for the last method.

Many of the mineral compounds used in the preparation of these colors are of a poisonous nature, which is a great drawback to their use... [4]

Matching Colors

There can be no "one-method" for matching the finish of an old piece. Some amount of experimentation must be undertaken; comparing the results with the sample to be duplicated. That said, there are currently some very good products on the market which can yield pleasing results. The best of these products will likely be found in specialty wood working stores and artist supply shops. I have always found the best success with these products when able to browse through a physical store location. Catalog shopping may be best done after gaining some familiarity with the basics.

A variety of methods have been used to alter the natural color of woods: dyes from natural sources, aniline stains (both water and alcohol soluble), and a number of caustic solutions. Our focus shall be on the methods deemed to be of a *less* toxic nature, as no restoration project is worth the risk of exposure to such dangers. Disposal of such things also presents further difficulties.

Many old wheels have markings (such as those on the uprights above) which may need color matching at times.

Artist supplies have replaced many of the old solvents with products which are gentler on Mother Earth, and much safer for the health of the finisher. Where turpentine and other driers are mentioned the reader is encouraged to seek out these more environmentally friendly options.

Burnt Umber and Raw Sienna are two important pigments for the restorer. While pigment stains are simple to mix, go easy on the amounts. Too much pigment, powdered, or oil can cause the grain to be hidden. A color chart is a handy item for reference.

CAUTION: *Always wear a respirator and gloves when using any powdered pigment or dye.*

Oil Stains

Color matching—small areas—may be accomplished with the use of common artist pigments and oil paints. Most colors may be obtained by combining some of the basic shades until a match is found:

-Raw Sienna
-Burnt Sienna
-Raw Umber
-Burnt Umber
-Van Dyke Brown

Desired color is added to a blend of :

3 parts boiled linseed oil
1 part turpentine
½ part Japan drier

Several shades of red are found useful if going for a Mahogany color; I also like to have a black on hand as well. The amount of base color to start with is a bead about as long as the width of your thumb. More is easier to add than less.

I like to use an 8-oz. glass mason jar (with a lid) for combining the oil, pigment, and turpentine. If drying seems overly long a little extra Japan drier can be used. Make sure to test the color and drying time first—before staining your piece. If the finish takes more than two days to dry, or feels tacky, thin with more boiled linseed and turpentine.

Priming the wood first, with: 1 part boiled linseed oil, 3 parts turpentine, can be useful to keep the pigment shade consistent. This is especially helpful around areas of end grain.

Recipes

Oak Stain— Begin with Raw Sienna for a base color. For dark wood add a little Burnt Umber; for lighter shades use Raw Umber instead.

Walnut Stain— Begin with Burnt Umber as a base color. Brownish shades may be obtained by adding a bit of Van Dyke Brown.

For a redder shade— Substitute a small bit of Burnt Sienna in place of the Van Dyke.

A much lighter shade— Add Raw Umber instead. Start with about one half as much Raw Umber, as Burnt Umber, and work up to the color needed.

Another— Vandyke Brown, lightened up as needed with Sienna.

Cherry Stain— Use Burnt Sienna as a base; add Raw Sienna to lighten if needed. (3 parts Burnt Sienna, 2 parts Raw Sienna).

Mahogany Stain— Raw Sienna in beer, add Burnt Sienna to find desired shade.

For a brownish shade— Mix: 3 parts Burnt Sienna, 1 part Rose Pink, 1 part Vandyke Brown

A reddish shade— Same as above, except: use 2 parts Rose Pink with the Burnt Sienna, and leave out the Van Dyke Brown.

Darkening Oak—Iron filings and vinegar is good for tight grained woods. The basic solution is made by dissolving iron filings in vinegar. (This is also a very old method of "blacking" leather.)

Another— A solution of green walnut shells can be very effective, using alum as a mordant. Take care to observe the shade; it may get too dark.

Antiquing Oak

Vandyke Brown or Lamp Black in oil. A variation of this may be done by staining a filler. Mix 1 part of color, to 4 parts filler; first mix Van Dyke brown and Lamp Black in equals parts, then add to the filler. Charcoal may be used in place of the Lamp Black.

Another— 4 parts Raw Sienna, 2 parts Burnt Umber, ½ part Lamp Black.

Basic Colors for Stains (in Liquid Parts)					
Shades	Yellow	Orange	Red	Dark Blue *	Black *
Light Oak	1	10	—	2	—
Golden Oak	—	22	1	3	—
Dark Oak	2	10	—	5	—
Light Walnut	—	12	1	—	4
Medium Walnut	—	14	1	—	6
Brown Mahogany	1	18	—	4	—
* Dark colors should be added last.					

SOURCE: Popular Mechanics Press, *Painting, Furniture Finishing and Repairing* (Chicago: Popular Mechanics Co., 1943), 31

Using a System

While there are a myriad of pre-mixed colors today, the restorer may find that these must still be diluted or strengthened a bit to be useful. Usually an additional color—or two—will be needed to capture the exact shade needed.

Before beginning any matching job there are three important considerations to keep in mind:

—1. The species of wood to be finished has much to do with the final color.

—2. The application of a top coat may darken the color.

—3. Color of many finishes tends to darken with time, and exposure to sunlight.

Selecting a base shade, to apply these rules to, may be approached in a systematic manner. The investment in time shall save the restorer much greater time than if it were not used.

Begin by selecting a small scrap board, of the same type to be used in the project, along with a base color. Now, mix up a solution which is obviously darker than what appears necessary. Make 10 progressive dilutions of this shade; until one is found which looks to be the shade needed. Pencil a number on the sample board next to the corresponding dilution sample. Set the board aside and allow the finish to dry.

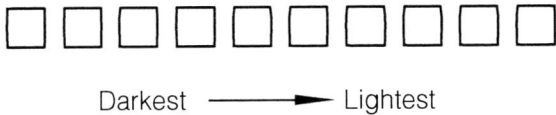

Darkest ⟶ Lightest

Single color test board, working from dark to light with each sample.

Record keeping now becomes important if the shades are to be reproduced accurately. The percentage of the diluting agent used, as well as the percentage of the base shade, should be measured as accurately as possible. If measuring powdered pigments a precision scale should be at hand. Liquid measures may be done with a graduated measure, used by chemists, or a precise kitchen measure. A conversion table of the various measurements used may be found on page 82.

Often it will be necessary to mix more than one color to obtain just the right shade for a match. A similar system, using a decreasing dilution of the color, is still the recommended method. The following illustrates two color matching:

Using two colors (or shades), the second sample is prepared in the same manner as before. A few more scrap boards are needed; for this example ten total are used. Positioning the 10 boards to form a square (see below) the first color dilutions are duplicated working darkest color at left, and the dilutions in progression to the right. Repeat this for each of the ten boards. Allow the samples to dry completely before continuing.

With the first samples dry, the second color (or shade) is brushed over the first sample. This time start at the upper left corner of the

First Color

Darkest ──────► Lightest

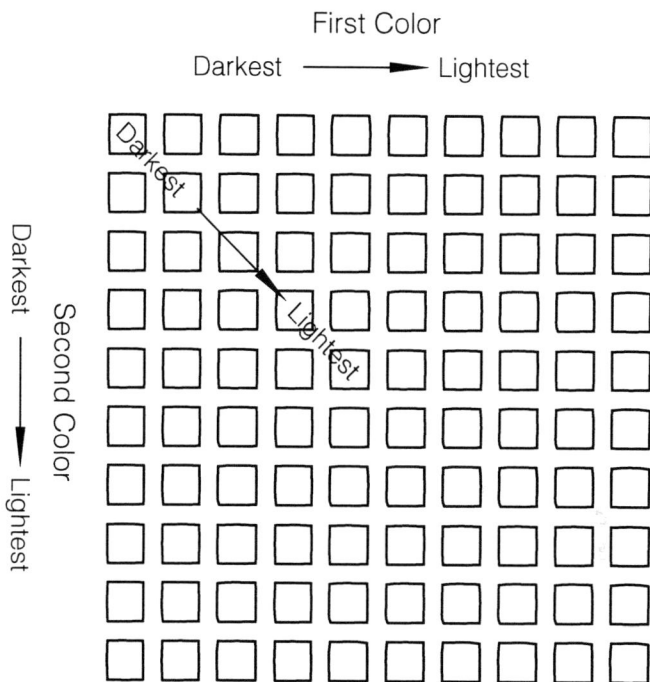

The two color system of color matching.

grid; begin as before with the darkest shade of the second color. Now working top to bottom, the progressive dilutions of the second color are laid over the first from left to right with each diluted sample. The result is 100 unique shades to choose from.

Once a suitable shade has been found don't forget to add any top coat to see how the color is affected. Make sure both the stain and any top coat have had a chance to completely dry. If time allows the sample should be left exposed to sunlight for a week or so, to judge the effects on darkening. This especially important if an oil finish has been chosen for the top coat.

Wax Finishes

Sometimes just giving a wheel a bit of polish will help blend in any new parts. Imitating the patina of age can also be aided by adding a bit of color to the wax. Detailed turnings (such as found on wheels) accumulate dust and old wax over time. Adding a bit of household dust to the compound, before waxing newly made parts, can also help simulate aging.

A fine wax is made by combining 1/2 pound beeswax, 1/2 pint turpentine, and 1/2 pint boiled linseed oil. The turpentine itself is adequate to melt the beeswax, albeit slowly. A quicker method is: melting the wax in a pan set in heated water; then—*after removing from the fire*—add the turpentine. Store the mixture in a tightly closed jar as the turpentine will otherwise evaporate away. Before using, warm the mixture in a pan filled with warm water to soften it up

Darkening the color obtained with this wax is easy. One very old method is: add 2 drams of alkanet root (source info in back) to every 20 ounces of turpentine[5] or linseed oil. The root is pounded until it shreds and put in a cloth bag (a tea holder works also), then placed in either the turpentine or the linseed oil. Remove the alkanet when the medium has reached the desired color.

Common Alkanet
Anchusa Officinalis

Another method of darkening the wax is by adding a bit of Burnt Umber. As with the stains, start with just a little; you can always add more if needed. Lamp Black may be used for a darker shade; chimney soot is a tolerable substitute (and much more affordable).

Lemon Oil Polish

Take ½ oz. oil of lemon and mix into 1 qt. of neutral oil: olive, mineral, or such. Apply sparingly; after 15-30 minutes buff with a soft cloth.

Dealing with Painted Wheels

Special caution should be taken in regards to painted wheels. Many an old paint recipe included lead as a primary ingredient.

The following from a 1917 paint manual applies to removing these old paints today as much as it did for the painters it was meant for then:

"Many pigments are poisonous, and the workman should be particularly careful to remove all paint stains from the skin, and not under any circumstances allow any of it to get into his mouth. A man should not eat in the same clothes in which he has painting, and before eating should not only change his clothes but wash all paint stains from his skin."[8]

Perhaps a better idea would be to leave those old painted wheels alone altogether.

Measures

APOTHECARIES' WEIGHT

Pound		Ounces		Drams		Scruples		Grains		Grams
1	=	12	=	96	=	288	=	5,760	=	373.24
		1	=	8	=	24	=	480	=	31.10
				1	=	3	=	60	=	3.89
						1	=	20	=	1.30
								1	=	.06

AVOIRDUPOIS WEIGHT

Pound		Ounces		Drams		Grains (Troy)		Grams
1	=	16	=	256	=	7,000	=	453.60
		1	=	16	=	437.5	=	28.35
				1	=	27.34	=	1.77

APOTHECARIES' WEIGHT

20 Grains	=	1 Scruple	=	20 Grains
3 Scruples	=	1 Dram	=	60 Grains
8 Drams	=	1 Ounce	=	480 Grains
12 Ounces	=	1 Pound	=	5,760 Grains

FLUID MEASURE

60 Minims	=	1 Fluid Dram
8 Drams	=	1 Fluid Ounce
16 ounces	=	1 Pint
8 Pints	=	1 Gallon

AVOIRDUPOIS WEIGHT

27 11-32 Grains	=	1 Dram	=	27 11-32 Grains
16 Drams	=	1 Ounce	=	437 ½ Grains
16 Ounces	=	1 Pound	=	7,000 Grains

Resources

Conservation supplies

Kremer Pigments
247 West 29th Street
New York, N.Y. 10001
(212) 219-2394
www.Kremerpigments.com
Old world quality pigments, resins, hide glues, shellacs.
When only the best will do.

Restoration Hardware & Finishes

Van Dyke's Restorers
P.O. Box 278
Woonsocket, SD 57385
(800)558-1234
www.Vandykes.com
A good range of ready-made finishes, milk paint, antiqued hardware and nails.

Tools, Finishes

Lee Valley Tools Ltd.
814 Proctor Avenue
Ogdensburg, NY 13669-2205
(800) 871-8158
www.Leevalley.com
Top shelf supplier of woodworking tools, quality finishes, antiqued hardware and square-cut nails.

Woodcraft
406 Airport Industrial Road
Parkersburg, WV 26102-1686
(800) 225-1153
www.Woodcraftsupply.com
Almost everything a woodworker could want is here. Of special interest for the wheel restorer are threading kits and polymerized linseed oil (the good kind).

Alkanet

Mountain Rose Herbs
P.O. Box 50220
Eugene, OR 97405
(800) 879-3337
www.Mountainroseherbs.com
Awesome selection of natural dye materials, roots, oils etc. When that old recipe calls for some strange root or herb and your organic food store never heard of it, these people probably have it.

Metals and Hardware

McMasterCarr
9630 Norwalk Blvd.
Santa Fe Springs, CA
90670-2932(562) 692-5911
www.Mcmastercarr.com
These guys have everything under the sun. A good source for leather bearing material, metals, whatever.

Machinist Tools, Reamers

Rutland Tool & Supply
111 E. Brokaw Rd.
San Jose, CA 95112
(408) 467-1500
www.Rutlandtool.com
Good overall selection of machinist tools. Range of pricing is likely to fit most pocketbooks.

Suggested Reading

Books

Spinning Wheels and Accessories
David A. Pennington
& Michael B. Taylor
Schiffer Publishing, Atglen, PA

Publications

The Spinning Wheel Sleuth
P.O. Box 422
Andover, MA 01810
www.spwhsl.com

Notes

Chapter One

1. A Society of Gentlemen in Scotland, *Encyclopedia Brittannica or A Dictionary of Arts and Sciences* (Edinburgh: A. Bell and Macfarquhar, 1771), Vol III, 621

2. Peter Kriedte, Hans Medick, Jürgen Schlumbohm Translated by Beate Schempp, *Industrialization Before Industrialization*, (Cambridge University Press, Cambridge, 1981), 163-164

3. Bergeron, L.-E., *The Turner's Manual : being a complete translation of the valuable work of L. E. Bergeron, with the improvements and alterations introduced up to the present time ; illustrated with fine woodcuts and lithographic engravings of the original plates, also of the various modern appliances ; being a perfect edition of the work of M. Bergeron, supplemented with original notes and appendices, necessary to render it a comprehensive encyclopædia of turning, plain and ornamental, in all its branches.* (London: Offen, 1877), 109

4. Joseph Moxon, *Mechanick Exercises : or the Doctrine of Handy-Works, Applied to the Arts of Smithing, Joinery, Carpentry, Turning & Bricklayery,* (London: Dan. Winter and Tho. Leigh, 1703), 190

5. John Horner, *The Linen Trade of Europe during the Spinning-Wheel Period* (Belfast: McCaw, Stevenson & Orr, 1920), 395

6. Ibid. 119

7. E. Lipson, *The History of the Woollen and Worsted Industries* (London: A.& C. Black, 1921), frontispiece

8. W. Cunningham, *The Growth of English Industry and Commerce During the Early and Middle Ages* (London: Cambridge University Press, 1890), 431

9. —, *The Swiss Family Robinson* (Chicago: Donohue, Henneberry & Co., 1899), 221

10. Lyster H. Dewey, *Yearbook of the United States Department of Agriculture 1913*, (Washington: Government Printing Office, 1914), 287-288

11. Ibid 296, 302

12. Ibid. 302, 287

13. Ibid 291

14. *A Dictionary of Arts and Sciences* 1771, Vol I, 686 - Vol II, 28

15. J. Matthews, *The Textile Fibres Their Physical, Microscopical and Chemical Properties* (New York: John Wiley and Sons, 1907), 326-328

16. *A Dictionary of Arts and Sciences* 1771, Vol III, 409

17. Pamela Goddard "Farnham Family Textile Tools." *The Spinning Wheel Sleuth* 10 (October 1995): 4-6

18. William Sandys and Simon Andrew Forster, *The History of the Violin* (London: John Russell Smith, 1864), 290, 292, 296, 209, 333, 343, 341

19. H.R. Fox Bourne, *The Life of John Locke* (New York: Harper and Brothers, 1876), 363-368

Chapter Two

1. George Horne, *The Duty of Contending for the Faith...* (London: F. & J. Rivington, 1788)

2. Samuel Record, *Identification of the Economic woods of the United States* (New York: John Wiley and Sons, 1919), Plate II, III,IV, V

3. A. D. Hopkins, T.E. Snyder, *Powder-Post Damage by Lyctus Beetles to Seasoned Hardwood, Farmer's Bulletin 778*, (Washington, D.C.: United States Department of Agriculture, 1917), 15-19

4. Sandor Nagyszalanczy, *Fixing and Avoiding Woodworking Mistakes* (Newtown, CT: Taunton Press, 1995), 58

5. J. S. Rogers and C. W. Beebe, *Leather Bookbindings How to Preserve Them, Leaflet No. 398*, (Washington: Govt. Printing Office, 1958), 4-5

6. H.R. Proctor, *The Making of Leather* (Cambridge: University Press, 1914), 88

7. Ibid, 144

8. Margaret S. Furry, *How to Prevent and Remove Mildew, Home and Garden Bulletin No. 68*, (Washington: Govt. Printing Office, 1960), 13

9. Allerton S. Cushman, *The Corrosion of Fence Wire, Farmers Bulletin No. 239*, (Washington: Govt. Printing Office, 1905), 7

10. John Erskine, P.H.D., Selections from Spenser's *The Faerie Queene* (New York: Longmans, Green, and Co., 1905), 3

11. Bradley Stoughton, *The Metallurgy of Iron and Steel*, (New York: Mc-Graw Hill Book Co., 1913), 66, 359

12. John L. Bacon, *Forge Practice and Heat Treatment of Steel* (Brooklyn, NY: John Wiley & Sons, 1919), 51-55

13. Moxon, *Mechanick Exercises*, 217

14. John G. Hawthorne & Cyril Stanley Smith, *Theophilus on Divers Arts, the Foremost Medieval Treatise on Painting, Glassmaking and Metalwork* (University of Chicago Press, 1963), 91
(Reprinted in 1979 by Dover Publications)

15. Edward H. Knight, *Knight's New Mechanical Dictionary* (Boston: Houghton, Mifflin and Co., 1884), 773

16. Chas A. Strelinger, *A Book of Tools, Machinery and supplies* (Detroit, MI: Chas A. Strelinger and Co., 1895), 142
(Reprinted in 1991 by Lindsay Publications)

Chapter Three

1. —, *Natural Woods and How to Finish Them* (Detroit: Berry Bros., Limited, Varnish Manufacturers, 1894), 10

2. Ralph Parsons Kinney, *The Complete book of Furniture Repair and Refinishing* (New York: Charles Scribner's Sons, 1950), 158

3. Popular Mechanics Press, *Painting, Furniture Finishing and Repairing* (Chicago: Popular Mechanics Co., 1943), 33-35

4. J. Merritt Matthews, *Application of Dyestuffs to Textiles, Paper, Leather and Other Materials* (New York: John Wiley and Sons, 1920) , 513

5. Fred T. Hodgson, *Hodgson's New Hardwood Finishing. Including Wood Manipulation Staining and Polishing* (Chicago: Frederick J. Drake and Co., 1904), 203

6. Percy H. Walker, *Use of Paint on the Farm, Farmer's Bulletin 474*, (Washington, D.C. 1917), 19

Index

Contents of other books in
The Wheel-Maker's Craft™ Series

Guide to Making Spinning Wheel Flyers and Wheels

ELEMENTS OF HANDSPINNING · Using the Wheel · Learning to Spin · WHEEL MECHANICS · Friction · Belt Drives · Flyer Design and Yarn Twist · MAKING FLYERS · Flyer Arms · Flyer Shaft · Bobbins · Whorls · WHEEL FABRICATION · Making a Six Segment Wheel · Drilling the Spoke Holes · Making the Hub · Making the Wheel Axle · Making the Crank Arm

Guide to Making

Spinning Wheel
Flyers and Wheels

Carson Cooper

Guide to Making Spinning Wheels, Plans and Instructions for Building Saxony, Irish Castle and Accelerator Wheels

BEFORE THE INDUSTRIAL AGE · MATERIALS · SAXONY · The Wheel Assembly · Drilling the Table Holes · Leg Angles · Upright Bearings · Making the Treadle · The Mother of All · Flyer Assembly · Whorl Groove Sizing · DOUBLE WHEEL ACCELERATOR · Making the Wheels · The Double Crank Arm · Making the Accelerator · Belt Tensioner for the Accelerator · Footman Assemblies · IRISH CASTLE · Tripod Assembly · Locating the Axle Holes · The Mother of All · HARDWARE FOR THE PROJECTS

Guide to Making
Spinning Wheels

Plans and Instructions for Building
Saxony, Irish Castle and
Accelerator Wheels

Carson Cooper

Cooper Smith Publishing

Manufactured in the United States of America